to
TALES
of
Philadelphia

forgotten TALES of Philadelphia

Thomas & Edward White

illustrations by

Karleigh Hambrick

Charleston — London

THE History PRESS

Published by The History Press

Charleston, SC 29403

www.historypress.net

First published 2011

Manufactured in the United States

ISBN 978.1.60949.270.0

Library of Congress Cataloging-in-Publication Data

White, Edward.

Forgotten tales of Philadelphia / Edward White and Thomas White.

p. cm.

Includes bibliographical references.

ISBN 978-1-60949-270-0

1. Philadelphia (Pa.)--History--Anecdotes. 2. Philadelphia Region (Pa.)--
History--Anecdotes. 3. Philadelphia (Pa.)--Social life and customs--Anecdotes. 4.
Philadelphia Region (Pa.)--Social life and customs--Anecdotes. 5. Philadelphia
(Pa.)--Biography--Anecdotes. 6. Philadelphia Region (Pa.)--Biography--
Anecdotes. 7. Curiosities and wonders--Pennsylvania--Philadelphia--History-
-Anecdotes. 8. Curiosities and wonders--Pennsylvania--Philadelphia Region--
History--Anecdotes. I. White, Thomas. II. Title.

F158.36.W45 2011

974.8'11--dc23

2011030026

For our wives, Heather and Justina

Acknowledgements

We would like to take this opportunity to thank everyone who helped us while we were writing this book, especially our wives, Heather and Justina, and children, Tommy and Marisa. We also want to thank our parents, Tom and Jean, for their continuous support. Michael Hassett, Therese Joseph, Paul Demilio and Elizabeth Williams expended considerable time and effort proofreading and editing this manuscript, and we are grateful for their help. Andrew Gable used his extensive knowledge of Pennsylvania oddities and unusual phenomena to point us in the direction of several interesting tales. His assistance is greatly appreciated. Many other people made important contributions to this book in one form or another and shared useful information, including Shane Frey, Gerard O'Neil, Ken Whiteleather, Vince Grubb, Brian Mckee, Kurt Wilson, Tony Lavorgne, Brett Cobbey, Dan Simkins and Brian Hallam. We would also like to thank Hannah Cassilly and the rest of the staff at The History Press for allowing us to write another volume in their "Forgotten Tales" series.

Introduction

It is not necessary to explain the historical significance of the city of Philadelphia and the important role that it has played in the development of the state of Pennsylvania and the United States as a whole. As the center of William Penn's "Holy Experiment" and the heart of the original thirteen colonies, the influence of the city and its people has impacted almost all facets of American society and culture. Numerous volumes have been written that analyze that impact and chronicle the growth of the city and the lives of its important figures. This is not one of them.

The focus of *Forgotten Tales of Philadelphia* is on stories that have generally been lost in the shadows of the larger events. This book is for those of us who enjoy reading about the bizarre and obscure parts of history. It is about the odd happenings, strange people, local legends and distant disasters that have added an element of character to the city over the centuries. In this volume you will find ghosts, legends, heroes, hoaxes, miracles, murders, rampaging animals and forgotten crimes. Some of these tales are humorous, some are tragic and others are just strange. From Nazi spies and grave robbers to a magnetic cloud and a flute-playing ghost, these tales cover a broad spectrum of the unusual. We hope that even those who are well versed in the history of the city will find something here that is new to them.

These tales have been gathered from a variety of sources. The only criteria that we used to select them were that they are relatively unknown to the average person and occurred within or just outside of Philadelphia. Often these accounts are derived from old newspapers or other obscure sources such as old or rare books. They are meant to be brief, and we attempted to track down and verify as many details as we could. Sometimes, because of the nature of the stories, certain facts remained elusive and are noted in the text as such. We hope that you find these unusual events and characters from Philadelphia's past as interesting and enjoyable as we did.

Forgotten Tales of Philadelphia

THE ABDUCTION OF CHARLEY ROSS

All too often today's media is filled with reports of children who are abducted or disappear. Even though the media has devoted much more time to such tragic occurrences since the 1970s, one of the first cases that was widely covered in the press happened a century before. On the first day of July in 1874, four-year-old Charley Ross was kidnapped from his Germantown home and was never found. The men who took Charley demanded payment for his safe return. The abduction is generally acknowledged to be the first kidnapping for ransom case in the United States.

That summer day, Charley and his six-year-old brother, Walter, were playing in their front yard when a carriage pulled up to the curb. The two men in the carriage were familiar to the boys because they had driven by several times in the previous days and given them candy. This time, the men asked the boys to get into the carriage with them, promising more candy and fireworks. (This case is believed to have inspired the phrase "Don't take candy from strangers.") The boys climbed in, and the carriage pulled away. Several minutes later, Charley started to cry and wanted to return home. The men stopped the carriage in front of a store and gave Walter twenty-five cents to go inside and purchase fireworks. When Walter entered the store, the men sped off with Charley. The boy would never be seen again. Walter was returned to his father, Christian Ross, who had not even realized the boys were missing. He mistakenly believed that they had gone to the neighbor's yard to play.

Two days after the abduction, Christian received a poorly written ransom note from the kidnappers. It warned him not to go to the police and stated that his son would be returned if he paid them a ransom. Several days later, a second note demanded $20,000 for Charley. The kidnappers believed that Christian Ross was a wealthy man. Christian had done quite well for many years, but after the financial panic of 1873, he had sunk into heavy debt. Not only did Christian consider it unethical to pay the kidnappers, but it was also nearly impossible for him to raise the necessary funds to do so. He had to notify the police. They advised him that he was doing the right thing in not paying the ransom because it would only set a bad precedent and endanger other children. The police also believed that the men would release the boy after it became clear that no money would change hands. Soon, word of the kidnapping leaked to the press, and the story became front-page news around the country. Charley's image and story were everywhere. Christian continued to try to communicate with the kidnappers through the newspaper, but their responses soon ended. It seemed that the kidnappers were unprepared for the attention that their actions brought. Friends of Charley's family and other wealthy Philadelphians offered to pay the ransom money and hired detectives to try to track down the culprits. Christian continued to search for Charley until his death in 1897, ultimately spending $60,000 in the process.

Several suspects came to police attention in December 1874 after a botched robbery attempt. Two men named William Mosher and Joe Douglas were shot after breaking into a home in New York. Mosher died immediately, but Douglas lingered long enough to confess to the kidnapping. Some accounts say that he also claimed that Charley was still alive but that only Mosher knew his location. Others say that he admitted that the boy was dead. Either way, Charley was never located. Both men were positively identified as the kidnappers by the young Walter Ross. A friend of William Mosher named William Westervelt was arrested the following year because the police believed that he also may have had some involvement in the abduction. Westervelt, who was a former Philadelphia police officer, was quickly sent to trial. Though no direct evidence was found to link him to the abduction, he was convicted on charges of conspiracy and given a six-year prison sentence. He denied having any knowledge regarding the whereabouts of Charley.

The Ross family's home was demolished in 1926. The Cliveden Presbyterian Church now stands on the site. In the decades after the kidnapping, numerous individuals came forward claiming to be Charley, but none was positively identified by Walter. Walter Ross died in 1943.

A GHOST IN CLIFTON HEIGHTS

The appearance of a mysterious phantom caused fear and suspicion among some residents of Clifton Heights in December 1885. At that time, the area was more rural and isolated than today. The ghost was first spotted by a prominent citizen and property owner named Thomas Grady. After dusk one evening, Grady was walking back to town from one of the wool mills that he owned along Darby Creek. As he crossed the creek and looked up the pathway ahead of him, the "phantom" appeared. Grady described it as extremely tall, dressed in a white sheet from head to toe and holding a tomahawk in its right hand. He watched the ghost move around for a few moments, and then it drifted back into the woods. After the ghost disappeared, Grady returned to town and the speculation began. Some of the more skeptical residents believed that a prankster was the source of the apparition. Others believed that it was the spirit of a dead Indian warrior because local lore held that the Clifton Heights area had once been an Indian burial ground. Isaiah Bowden, one of the area's oldest residents, claimed that the Indian ghost had been seen every twenty years since he was a child.

Over the next week, at least six more people reported meeting this strange ghost near the creek. One of the six, James Dowling, entered the woods surrounding the creek with his hunting dogs. At that point, he had not heard of the story of the mysterious ghost. The dogs picked up a strange trail and followed it to the edge of the creek. After crossing, they caught the trail again on the other side and ran slightly ahead of Dowling up a wooded hillside. Only a moment later, the dogs ran back to Dowling, shaking and whimpering, refusing to go any farther. Dowling did not wish to proceed and see what frightened the dogs. When he returned home, his story spread in the community. The local police investigated the sightings, but there are not any reports as to whether they ever found any more information or had any suspects.

A Bull Causes Chaos in the City

On the evening of August 10, 1921, a rampaging bull caused injury and panic in the city. The bull was one of twenty-seven cattle being driven from the West Philadelphia stockyards to Camden. Along the way, the drover and the cattle had to stop at a railroad crossing at Third and Willow Streets. As they waited, the bull saw the freshly painted red caboose of a Reading Railroad freight train pass by. The bull snorted and chased after

the train. It charged through miles of streets for nearly two hours. Five police cars and numerous officers pursued the bull, firing at least two hundred rounds at the enraged beast. All of the shots missed their target. At the apex of the confusion, a civilian named William Dunn made a terrible mistake in his attempt to bring down the bull. He fired four loads of buckshot from his shotgun that completely missed the animal. Instead, the rounds struck fifteen bystanders who were trying to get out of the way. Dunn was taken into custody and charged

with aggravated assault and battery. The rampaging bull was finally brought down by an unnamed World War I veteran who fired five shots into its head.

HEX MURDER OR SOMETHING ELSE?

In mid-January 1932, the body of thirty-one-year-old Norman Bechtel was discovered on a Philadelphia street. The young accountant and Mennonite church worker had been brutally murdered with a knife. His car, which was full of bloodstains, was discovered six miles away. Though homicide was sadly not uncommon in the city, something about this case set it apart.

Whoever had killed Bechtel had apparently known him well enough to be allowed into his car. With his first blow, the killer forcefully plunged a long, thin knife through Bechtel's overcoat, suit jacket and eyeglass case and into his heart. The murderer then withdrew the knife and stabbed the young man seven more times in the shape of a circle around his heart. At that point, Bechtel stumbled out of the vehicle and onto the ground. Detectives also discovered a set of mysterious cuts on the victim's face. A small, crescent-shape cut was made on each side of the forehead. From his hairline to his nose was another vertical slash. Running off the vertical cut were two horizontal cuts that each went in the direction of the crescent-shaped wounds and a diagonal cut that went across his forehead. Though all of the victim's valuable items had been taken, detectives feared that there was more to the crime than simple robbery. Some suspected that there may have been occult or ritual elements to the crime because of the bizarre nature of the wounds.

Just a few years earlier, the famous "Hex Murder" had taken place in York County. The subsequent trial and motivations for the killing brought unfavorable light on the medicinal and magical folk tradition of some of the Pennsylvania Germans. This folk tradition was known as powwow or *brauche*. Powwowers were viewed in the German community as healers, and Christian overtones dominated their work. They provided cures, relief of symptoms, protection from curses (hexes) and evil and good luck charms; located lost animals and people; and made attempts at predicting the future. These practices were carried out by using amulets, charms, prayers and ritualized objects. Many practitioners of powwow were feared as well as respected because of their ability to practice the darker form of *brauche* known as *hexerei*. These hex doctors could conjure malevolent forces to inflict harm or curse their enemies. During the "Hex Murder" trial, the media sensationalized the practice of powwowing, associating it with witchcraft and "backward" rural Germans. The case revolved around the murder of one powwower by another over the belief in hexes. John Blymire and his accomplices accidentally killed Nelson Rehmeyer while trying to make him remove an imagined hex. The coverage made many people in Pennsylvania more aware (and fearful) of this tradition. Against such a backdrop, one can see how the strange mutilations on Bechtel's body could lead authorities to suspect an occult connection. This approach was further reinforced when they discovered that Bechtel, who was obviously of German descent, grew up in the farming country around Boyertown, where powwowing was once common. The detective in charge of the investigation, Captain Harry Heanly, ordered a thorough search of the victim's apartment to see if any connection to occult activity could be discovered and possibly give them a lead. Heanly came up empty-handed, however. All that was found at Bechtel's residence were Mennonite books and pamphlets.

Despite the fact that no direct evidence of *hexerei* was found, the press quickly labeled the crime another hex murder based on the suspicions of the police. The mysterious crime remained unsolved for five years. Then, in mid-April 1937, the police managed to extract a confession after receiving a tip. The strange murder had nothing to do with hexes and the occult after all. Thirty-six-year-old William Jordan admitted that he, along with four accomplices (one being a woman), had killed Bechtel. The details of Jordan's confession were kept quiet, but he and his accomplices had been attempting to blackmail Bechtel. When he refused to cooperate, they killed him. The cuts on his head had no special significance.

A SEA CAPTAIN'S STRANGE TALE

When the British steamer *Mohican* arrived at the docks in Philadelphia, it brought with it a strange tale in addition to its usual cargo. It was late July 1904, and the ship had been at sea since it had left the port at Braila, Romania. Captain Urquhart, the commander of the vessel, relayed their bizarre encounter.

As the *Mohican* approached the Delaware breakwater, the captain and his crew experienced something that they would never forget. The sun had just gone down, and the seas were calm. As the skies grew dark, an unusual gray cloud appeared on the horizon. The cloud seemed to grow larger and larger as the ship approached. Urquhart soon realized that it reached several hundred feet from the water into the sky. Strange glowing lights began to surround the vessel as the *Mohican* penetrated the cloud. To the crew's horror, the ship began to glow as well. The hair on the sailors' bodies, including beards, stood straight up. Amid the confusion, Captain Urquhart tried to calm the crew, but when he ordered the men to move an anchor chain on the deck, the situation became even more surreal. The chains would not budge, as if something was pulling against the men. It was then that they realized that all of the metal on the ship was magnetized. Urquhart described the ship's compass as "spinning like an electric fan." Every metal tool and object was drawn to the deck and the hull.

Just when Urquhart thought that the experience could not get any more terrifying, it did. The *Mohican* had been in the cloud for about ten minutes at this point, and the crew was already frightened enough when they started to feel it. Every member of the crew began to have trouble moving. Their arms and legs became stiff, and most of the men struggled to breathe. An eerie silence fell over the ship. Captain Urquhart tried to speak to the crew but was unable. He later said, "I tried to talk, but the words refused to leave my lips. The density of the cloud was so great that it would not carry sound." For almost half an hour, the crew waited in silent terror, wondering what fate was about to befall them, until the *Mohican* emerged from the other side of the magnetic cloud. The glow gradually faded, and the crew began to move about as normal. Chains and tools on the deck were no longer magnetized. The unnerved crew watched their silent suppressor slowly fade off in the distance behind them as they headed for port.

He Killed the Mayor—On Paper

On December 3, 1910, a disturbed Frank Maus forced his way into the reception room at the office of Mayor John E. Reyburn. He stormed up to one of the mayor's aides, waving his arms wildly. According to the *New York Times*, he shouted, "The police are a lot of robbers. They ought to be cleaned out of City Hall. I want my naturalization papers, and I've

got to have them right away. Look here, is this the Mayor?" The wild-eyed man grabbed a piece of paper and a pencil and drew a quick sketch of a stick figure with a face. He then answered his own rhetorical question. "Yes, that's the Mayor, and I came here to kill him, see?" Maus then drew a line through the stick figure and stabbed the paper with the pencil. Though the mayor's staff was becoming worried, the police quickly arrived and took the man into custody. Mayor Reyburn was never near the angry man.

Is This Train Going a Little Fast?

The Congressional Limited train, which ran from Washington, D.C., to New York in the early twentieth century, regularly made two stops in Philadelphia. On February 6, 1907, it was passing through on its usual run. Just after it departed from its stop in West Philadelphia, the train's fireman, Harry Michner, noticed that the train seemed to be accelerating rapidly. As it flew through Fairmont Park and approached its North Philadelphia stop, he knew that there was a problem. He called up to engineer Joseph Toms, but there was no response.

Michner climbed over the boiler rig and made his way to the engineer's cab. To his horror, he discovered that

Toms was dead and his corpse was leaning on the throttle. He had apparently been leaning out the window when his head struck an object along the tracks and was crushed. Michner was able to shift the body just in time to bring the train to a screeching halt at the North Philadelphia station, averting further tragedy.

The Jersey Devil Comes to Philadelphia

Few supernatural legends are as well known throughout America as that of the Jersey Devil. The horrific creature was allegedly born in the Pine Barrens of southern New Jersey sometime in 1735. The accounts of the creature's origins vary in detail, but most claim that the beast was the thirteenth child of "Mother Leeds." Leeds, who was rumored to practice witchcraft, was already struggling to support her other children. According to legend, while giving birth she said something to the effect of, "I'm tired of children, let this one be a devil." Other versions of the legend say that Leeds was cursed by a minister whom she had wronged or that the mother was actually a Mrs. Shourds who gave birth at Leed's Point. However it happened, the baby quickly transformed into a monster with a horse-like face, bat wings, claws and hooves. It shrieked angrily and flew out the chimney and into the Barrens, where it has made its home ever since.

In the years since its birth, the Jersey Devil has been seen by a variety of witnesses throughout New Jersey and Pennsylvania. Napoleon Bonaparte's older brother Joseph even claimed to have seen the creature while hunting in 1820. It has reportedly been shot at and hit numerous times but is unaffected. Sightings of the mysterious creature have often occurred in clusters. One particular wave of dozens of sightings happened in 1909. It was during that time that the creature appeared to residents of Philadelphia.

The most dramatic of those sightings occurred on Ellsworth Street in January. Mrs. J.H. White went out to her backyard clothesline at about four o'clock in the afternoon when she noticed something crouching in the corner of the yard. As she moved closer to see what it was, the Jersey Devil rose to its cloven feet and began to spit fire. Mrs. White later described the creature as being six feet tall and having skin like an alligator. The woman screamed in terror and then passed out. Alerted by the screams, Mr. White raced to the backyard only to find his wife on the ground and the gruesome creature spitting fire. He grabbed a pole and chased the Devil out of his yard and into an alley that connected to Sixteenth Street. He then stopped the chase and turned back to help his wife. The Jersey Devil was then seen by a witness on Sixteenth Street near Washington Avenue. Later that week, other residents reported seeing the legendary beast around the city. William Becker claimed to have pelted the Devil with rocks after he saw it on Lime Kiln Pike. Numerous others witnessed the creature on Beach Street at the intersection with Fairmont Avenue.

As the year progressed and more sightings were reported throughout New Jersey, the Philadelphia Zoo decided to offer a $10,000 reward to anyone who could capture the creature, provided that it really looked as it had been described. The building public interest/mass hysteria caused by the sightings also attracted hoaxers. Two of the most famous were residents of Philadelphia. Norman Jeffries, the public relations man for the Ninth and Arch Street Museum, and Jacob Hope, an animal trainer, came up with a scheme to make a profit off the Jersey Devil sightings. The men claimed that they had captured the creature but that it had escaped near Lee Street. They offered a $500 reward for the safe return of the Devil. Their "Jersey Devil" was actually a kangaroo with fake bat wings attached. The pair found some local men and dressed them as farmers. The men "captured" the beast so that the press would cover the story and pictures could be taken. Almost immediately, the creature was taken to the Ninth and Arch Street Museum and put on display. Curious spectators could see the "Leeds Devil" for a ten-cent entrance fee. An advertisement describing the show described the creature as "The Fearful, Frightful, Ferocious Monster

Which Has been Terrorizing Two States." Twenty years later, Jeffries admitted to the hoax and described it in detail for the *Philadelphia Record*. Even so, numerous other sightings could not be explained away easily for those who believed. If anything, the popularity of the Jersey Devil has increased in the years since. Sightings of the Devil have continued sporadically in both states even today.

SINGER FORESEES HER OWN DEATH

Margaret Williamson, a thirty-two-year-old divorcée, was beginning to enjoy a career as a professional vocalist. She had studied in Europe for a while and by 1925 enjoyed a growing reputation as a fine singer. Despite her youth and success, in March of that year she felt as if her life was about to come to an end. She confessed her premonition to some friends on March 26. Though their reactions were not recorded, they did help her select music for her funeral. Williamson also contacted an undertaker and made all of the other necessary arrangements the following day. On the evening of March 27, Williamson was again entertaining her friends in her studio when she suddenly fell ill. They rushed her to the hospital, and she died there only a few hours later. The doctors could find no clear cause of death. She had simply slipped away.

THE FIRST AMERICAN CIRCUS

The first circus to perform in America was formed by John Bill Ricketts in Philadelphia in 1792. While not as sensationalized as circuses would later become with the exploits of P.T. Barnum, the show was a new and unique form of live entertainment for the young country. It combined theatrical performances with daring equestrian acts. Ricketts came to Philadelphia from England in the fall of 1792 and began training horses in a hastily constructed circus building at Twelfth and Market Streets. The wooden building was essentially an arena constructed around a ring that was forty-two feet in diameter. It had no roof, and all of his performances occurred during daylight hours. The first public performance occurred on April 3, 1793. Ricketts performed tricks such as juggling while riding backward on a horse and riding two horses at once, standing with a foot on each. The show quickly became popular, and even President George Washington attended one performance on April 24. (The two became friends, and Ricketts even put on a special performance when Washington left office.) By July, Ricketts decided to take his show on the road, traveling to New England and up and down the East Coast. He returned to Philadelphia in September and began construction on a newer, better circus facility.

The new building (which had a roof), called Ricketts' Art Pantheon and Amphitheater, opened in October with additional acts that included acrobats, clowns, a tightrope walker and pantomimes. It was located at the intersection of Chestnut and Sixth Streets. Over the next few years, Ricketts expanded his circus and profited from a lack of competition. His success made him a celebrity, and everyone wanted tickets to his shows. Despite its success, the circus came to an end in 1799 due to a devastating accident. An unattended candle started a fire in the circus building that completely destroyed the structure. The financial impact was devastating for Ricketts. He made one final attempt to reestablish his show in another building in 1800, but the new show was unsuccessful. Ricketts eventually sold his horses to recover his losses and then set sail for England. His ship was lost at sea with no survivors.

CURSE LIFTED AFTER THIRTY-TWO YEARS

In 1876, twenty-eight-year-old Dennis Comey was living in a Philadelphia boardinghouse run by sixty-two-year-old Mary Costello. Comey performed manual labor for a living, so his income was never stable. When he lost his job, he decided to leave the boardinghouse without paying the ninety dollars that he owed in rent. Needless to say, Mrs. Costello did not take the news well. As Comey was walking out, she dropped to her knees and called down numerous curses upon the man. Comey did not take the curses seriously and was on his way.

Over three decades later, Comey inherited a large sum of money. Somehow, Mary Costello, who was now ninety-four years old, found out about his good fortune. She lived in Atlantic City at that time but attempted to collect the money that Comey still owed her. Comey agreed to pay, but with one condition. Mrs. Costello had to lift the curse that she had placed on him decades before. Costello signed a document that read:

> *Know all men by these present that I, Mary Costello, do hereby revoke, recall, and retract to the utmost of my power the curse which Dennis Comey claims that I put on him in 1876, calling down upon him and his, as he claims, ill-luck, disease, and disaster through life and eternity, living and dead, at all times from the present to the end of the world, even unto the tenth generation, and do hereby declare that I hold for him nothing but sentiments of good will and respect.*

Comey received the document and then traveled to Atlantic City. Mrs. Costello verbally reiterated the contents of the document. Comey, apparently being a bit of a jerk at that point, tried to get the old woman to apologize on her knees. Costello's family and friends refused to allow that to happen. Comey finally paid his ninety-dollar bill.

THEY BURIED THE WRONG MAN

By late February 1878, Daniel O'Neill had been missing for several weeks. He was a bricklayer by trade, but his family had not been able to find him working at any construction site in Philadelphia. On February 24, his brother Patrick read a notice in the *Philadelphia Record* about a man who had been struck and killed by a train on the tracks of the Pennsylvania Railroad in Camden. The description of the dead man seemed to match his brother. Initially, Patrick went to Camden and positively identified the mangled remains as Daniel. The next day, their sister and Daniel's wife and family arrived and also positively identified the remains. The body was transported back to Philadelphia, but no wake was held because of its condition. After a funeral Mass, the body was buried in the cathedral cemetery.

Two days later, while the family grieved, Daniel O'Neill walked back into his brother's house. Needless to say, they were shocked. For a few moments, they thought that a miracle had occurred and that Daniel had come back from the dead. Word quickly spread throughout the neighborhood about the miracle, but it was soon learned that the cause of Daniel's reappearance was much more mundane. He had been in Wilmington, Delaware, allegedly selling matches. It is not known why he did not tell his family where he was, and their joy quickly turned to anger. Somehow they had all misidentified the body in Camden (and paid for the burial).

The *Philadelphia Record* Tests Wartime Security

In the early months of the Second World War, the government and public alike feared sabotage and infiltration by Axis agents. As the war effort picked up momentum, any manufacturing or military facility could be a potential target. The naval shipyard and docks of Philadelphia were some of those many vital facilities. Two editors of the *Philadelphia Record* wondered how safe these sites were, so they decided to put wartime security to a rather direct test. William B. Mellor Jr. and Frank Toughill had heard that a pair of British reporters had walked around a London suburb in Nazi uniforms and were not stopped or questioned. The editors thought that they should attempt the same thing on the docks in their city. Dressed as German naval officers with swastika armbands, the two reporters wandered around the docks and downtown Philadelphia. The pair spoke with false German accents, pointed at defense facilities and navy ships and even asked a traffic cop for directions. The only person who bothered to stop them was a police officer. He only wanted to write them a ticket for being illegally parked. However, when the officer realized that they were in the "navy," he tore up the citation. A few moments later, a young boy on roller skates passed them and said, "Oh boy! Join the navy and see the world." *Time* magazine cited the incident in its February 9, 1942 issue as a warning against lax security.

Nazi Spies Arrested

Speaking of wartime espionage, a pair of Nazi spies was arrested at the docks in 1945. The two men, both Spaniards, were dragged out of their beds on the freighter SS *Manuel Calvo* after it had reached the city on the morning of June 23. Thirty-three-year-old Pablo Meso Lagaretta and twenty-seven-year-old Emilio Ipes Cazua Hernandes had been under surveillance by the Federal Bureau of Investigation for two years as they passed information back to their spymaster in Spain.

Observation of the pair began after another Spaniard, Jose Laradogoitia, walked into the FBI's New York office in 1943. Laradogoitia had slipped away from a freighter in Philadelphia a few days earlier. He had also been recruited and trained as a spy by Nazi agent George Lang while in his home country. His mission was to gather general intelligence, as well as information on American designs and plans for jet aircraft. Laradogoitia had a change of heart, however, and decided to tip off the Americans.

Laradogoitia provided the FBI with a counterespionage opportunity. They asked him to become a double agent, and he agreed. Until the end of the war, the FBI set up a short-wave radio for Laradogoitia to broadcast false information to the rest of the spy network. Hernandes and Lagaretta served as couriers, passing information and payments between Lang and Laradogoitia. Hernandes would hide rolls of money in his mouth (sometimes as much as $2,100) and deliver it to Laradogoitia as payment. Lagaretta would tape secret documents, maps and blueprints to his body and smuggle them back to Spain.

When the Germans surrendered, communications from Lang stopped. At that point, the FBI decided to move in and arrest the couriers when their ship arrived in Philadelphia. When the men were brought to trial, they could have faced the death penalty. Instead, they were given ten-year sentences since they were merely go-betweens. Hernandes revealed that he was only paid $750 for his participation. He claimed that he was pressured because he was engaged to the daughter of another agent and feared that he would not be allowed to marry her if he refused.

TRAINS COLLIDE IN TUNNEL

On May 17, 1900, a horrific and preventable accident occurred in the Baltimore and Ohio Railroad tunnel that ran under Twenty-fifth Street between Callowhill Street and Fairmont Park. That evening, the New York freight express was making its usual run through the tunnel. Since the tunnel was semicircular, with a steep grade, the engine would pull the cars through in two sections before reattaching them. On that occasion, seventeen of the forty-three cars were left standing halfway through the dark tunnel as they waited for the first section to be pulled through. This should not have been a problem because the tower operator, Frank Lamtell, was supposed to switch the white "all clear" light to red to warn oncoming trains to stop. Things did not go as planned because Lamtell fell asleep on the job. At 11:30 p.m., a train approached at about thirty miles per hour. George Laub, the engineer on the oncoming train, saw the white light and picked up speed. Once he had entered the tunnel, it was too late. The accelerating train plowed into the stopped cars with tremendous force. Laub and his fireman, George Blackman, were killed on impact. It was later discovered that five vagrants, described as "tramps," had been in one of the cars and were also killed in the collision. Both trains were quickly engulfed in flames, and three oil cars exploded. Firemen arrived to fight the inferno, but they were quickly overcome by smoke in the tunnel. They were forced to knock holes through the street above to vent the smoke. It took many hours to extinguish the flames, and almost thirty firemen received minor injuries. Lamtell initially fled the scene after realizing what had happened but soon returned and surrendered to authorities, accepting full blame for the tragedy.

The Phantom Flutist

One lonely night in December 1885, Patrolman Carroll of the Darby police force made an unsettling discovery during his nightly patrol. Carroll was on high alert due to a recent murder, and he was looking out for any nefarious characters. He came upon the Darby jail at 11:00 p.m. and heard someone playing the flute on the second floor. Carroll knew that the second floor was

empty, and he shivered with fear at the sound of the phantom music. The officer un-holstered his gun and grabbed his club as he crept up the stairs to the second floor. When he reached the top, Carroll crouched down and spied through the peephole a vision of an elderly man with large funny eyes, a huge mouth and crooked legs. The strange phantom was playing a beautiful rendition of "Climbing up the Golden Stairs" on a flute. The flutist's eyes increasingly grew larger as Carroll looked on. Unfortunately, Carroll made a noise as he fell against the door, and the flutist abruptly disappeared. The flutist reappeared and continued to play undisturbed every night because Carroll had decided to enjoy the music from down the street. Carroll was quoted as saying that this was "the greatest mystery I ever knew of." Patrolman Carroll, who served as the "Chief of Police, Lieutenant, Sergeant, and lone patrolman of the Darby Police Force," had a reputation for being "a sober, conscientious man, and the story of the ghost in the village lock-up is generally believed from one end of Darby to the other." Many of the villagers started locking their doors and carrying firearms to repel any unwanted flutists from entering their homes (though we're not sure how that would stop a ghost). It is not clear how long the phantom flutist continued to make his presence known.

THE KENSINGTON TORNADO

On April 12, 1856, a treacherous twister hit the Kensington section of Philadelphia and caused much confusion and chaos across the rest of the city. The tornado only lasted between ten and fifteen minutes, but it caused more than $100,000 in damages throughout the area. At ten o'clock at night, violent winds started, which were accompanied by lightning and a large hailstorm. A funnel cloud soon followed.

There were a total of nine serious injuries reported in Kensington, but no fatalities. In one instance, two children of James May were buried underneath bricks as they lay sleeping in their bed. The Mays' house was destroyed after debris from a Presbyterian church struck their home and caused the roof to cave in. The children were injured, but the other nine occupants of the home escaped unscathed.

The tornado capsized a cargo ship docked on the Delaware River while five of its crew members were still on board. The captain and two members of the crew held onto a flour barrel and some planks and made it to shore. The rest were found clinging onto the wreckage after the tornado had stopped. In total, 224 homes, 6 churches, 2 train stations, 8 shops and 14 factories were damaged, and 5 homes, 4 factories, 3 stables and a slaughterhouse were completely destroyed.

PANIC AT THE CIGAR FACTORY

A non-lethal accident with an elevator at the Harburger, Homan & Co. Cigar factory (owned by the American Tobacco Company) resulted in a deadly panic that claimed several lives in 1902. A deaf and mute young man named Isador Baccus worked as the janitor in the five-story building that was located at Tenth Street and Washington Avenue. On April 30, while performing his duties on the fourth floor, he realized that he needed to retrieve a ball of twine from the fifth floor. Baccus went over to the manually operated elevator and began to pull on the rope to bring it to his level. He was leaning into the shaft to see where it was when the carriage came down from above him and landed on the back of his head and neck. The weight of the elevator pinned his head and body to the floor. A nearby stock boy ran over and freed Baccus, calling for help. The factory foreman quickly ran out of the building to get an ambulance. Unfortunately, while he was gone, panic erupted among the nearly 1,200 women who worked in the building rolling cigars and operating equipment.

Several of the young women who heard the cries for help thought that there was a fire. The rumor spread in minutes as girls, some as young as twelve, leapt from their workplaces and rushed to the stairwell to escape. The crowds pushed their way down to a bend between the second and third floors. At that point, the women in the front of the line tripped and blocked the stairs. Some other workers tripped over the women or just stepped on them trying to escape the nonexistent fire. A few young women, realizing that the stairs were blocked, leapt from the windows, some as high as fifty feet. One twelve-year-old girl was killed instantly by the fall.

The girls' screams could be heard a block away in every direction, and the fire company was alerted. When the firemen entered the building with police, they attempted to calm the panicked workers. However, seeing the firemen initially made the panic worse. It made the women think that there was indeed a fire, so they pushed harder to escape. Police and firemen outside tried to calm anyone who approached the upstairs windows to keep them from jumping. Finally, rescuers reached the women who had been trampled and injured in the stairwell. So many workers had sustained injuries that police could not find enough ambulances, and nearby wagons had to be commandeered. Frightened relatives from the surrounding neighborhood arrived on the scene, making it more difficult for rescuers to work. By the time the panic had subsided, eight were dead, three were critically injured and numerous others were bruised and battered. Most of the dead were eighteen years old or younger.

GRAVE ROBBERS

In the 1800s and earlier, it was very difficult for doctors and surgeons to obtain human bodies that could be used for teaching and experimentation. Though almost everyone wanted well-trained physicians, very few people were willing to have their corpse cut apart for the sake of science. This shortage forced some doctors to resort to illegal methods to obtain bodies. Some would pay for corpses with no questions asked. Others commissioned petty criminals to dig up freshly buried bodies. Occasionally, these doctors and their accomplices would get caught, and accounts of their misdeeds would be carried in newspapers and periodicals in Europe and the Americas.

Philadelphia had its own case of body-snatching doctors. Several investigative reporters uncovered a grave-robbing operation in the city in 1882. Led by Louis Megarge, editor of the *Philadelphia Press*, the reporters monitored the thieves for eight months as they came and went from Lebanon Cemetery. Finally, after securing enough evidence, Megarge called in a Pinkerton detective named William Henderson on December 4. They caught Levi Chew and his brother Robert with a wagon full of six recently buried corpses. The men, who were both related to the cemetery superintendent, would quietly take their wagon into the back part of the burial ground late at night and dig up bodies. The Chew brothers were helped by another man named Frank McNamee, who was also arrested. McNamee confessed the details of the entire plot to the press and to the police.

According to McNamee, the men had actually been hired by Dr. William Forbes, a prominent physician and instructor of anatomy at Jefferson Medical College. Three years before the arrest, an assistant to Dr. Forbes named Dr. Behan had approached McNamee about acquiring the bodies. At first, McNamee had retrieved a few bodies from the jail on the doctor's behalf, but then another assistant, Dr. Lohman, had taken him to the cemetery at night to meet the Chew brothers. After the sun went down, the brothers dug up the bodies of those who had just been interred. Lohman and McNamee then took the corpses back to the college. He continued do this for the next three years. At first, McNamee was paid one dollar for each body, but later he made as much as three dollars per body. The Chew brothers were paid between five and eight dollars per corpse. Sometimes McNamee was assisted by another man named Henry Pillet. McNamee claimed that he thought that the college was legitimately entitled to the bodies and did not think he was breaking the law. The crime caused particular outrage in the city's African American community because the bodies were taken from a black cemetery. Angry mobs of African American residents assembled at the magistrate's office and later the courthouse when the men were arraigned and put on trial. Some brought razor blades, knives and pistols, determined to see justice done one way or another. The Chew brothers, Pillet and McNamee were all convicted and each received a ten-year prison sentence. The police then arrested Dr. Forbes and Dr. Lohman.

At his trial, Forbes admitted that he had received as many as 150 bodies a year from McNamee but claimed that he did not know where they had originated. His attorney called up numerous character witnesses that supported the doctor's reputation. It was claimed that he was, at worst, guilty of bad judgment in not questioning the source of the bodies. Forbes was acquitted of all criminal charges. The charges against Dr. Lohman were dropped before he went to trial.

POLICEMAN SACRIFICES LIFE TO SAVE CHILDREN

On May 8, 1910, Officer William Weiss was working at an outdoor circus performance that included a race. Four chariots, each with a team of four horses, were racing around a long track at the circus grounds. On their final lap, three small children tried to cross the track, oblivious to the danger that they were in. All four chariots were barreling down on them, and the horses were going too fast to stop in time. Officer Weiss darted onto the track and pushed the children to safety just in time. The first two chariots were able to swerve and avoid Weiss, but the third had nowhere to go. The brave officer was knocked down and trampled under the horses' hooves. He did not survive his injuries, but the three children were safe.

THE BLOB THAT FELL FROM THE SKY

Two Philadelphia police officers witnessed a strange occurrence one night while on patrol in 1950. It was September 26, and Officers John Collins and Joe Keenen were making their usual rounds in their car when they spotted a "shimmering object" drop from the sky into a nearby field. The officers decided that they should investigate the fallen object, so they drove to the edge of the field and exited their car. As the officers approached the landing site, a bad stench permeated the air. It seemed to be coming from the location of the impact. When their flashlight beams finally landed on the object, the officers were shocked. It appeared to be a large gelatinous blob, about six feet in diameter and one foot thick. Collins was quoted as saying, "It looked like it was alive." As the pair turned away from the blob to call for backup and turned their flashlights off, they realized that it actually had a faint purple glow. A few moments later, Sergeant Joe Cook and Officer James Cooper arrived.

They suggested that someone try to pick it up. Collins attempted to do this, but the material broke apart in his hands as if it were jelly. The situation became even stranger when the few pieces that stuck to his hand soon evaporated, leaving behind only a sticky residue. Within hours, the rest of the blob suffered a similar fate. The officers were never able to determine exactly what the substance was.

THE MAN WHO LIVED IN A BOILER

An article in the *New York Times* in March 1885 told the story of a strange old man who lived in a boiler. The man's story came to light because he testified in Judge Yerkes's courtroom against a young man who was charged with assaulting and robbing him in his "home." The man, whose name was Joseph Hance, was described as looking like "Father Time," with a long gray beard and long gray hair. He wore tattered clothes and carried an old walking stick.

Hance lived in an old iron boiler that was located in a vacant lot at Otsego and Mifflin Streets. He said that in the winter he closed up the ends with wood, and that he had been living in it since his wife had died years before. He stated in court, "I want only to be let alone. Why can't I be let alone in my poor boiler?" Hance testified that a young man named Patrick McClosky broke into his boiler, beat him and then stole his coat after trying to steal his food. McClosky was arrested the following day.

Hance managed to recover his coat, which had been sold to a secondhand store the same day as the robbery. McClosky had sold it for twelve cents. Judge Yerkes found the young man guilty and sentenced him to eighteen months in prison. Hance returned to his boiler to live in obscurity.

THE TEN-MINUTE STRIKE

In early January 1905, the young women who worked the telephone switchboards for the Keystone Company decided to go on strike. They had recently been notified by the assistant superintendent of wires, Harry Jacquett, that the half-day off that they received every other Saturday was being rescinded. The ladies would now have to work a full shift every weekend. All of the operators signed a petition to have the half-day restored, but it was ignored by management. The women decided to take matters into their own hands.

At 8:20 a.m. on January 7, one hundred women at the main exchange and one hundred more at another exchange got up, gathered their things and began filing out. Harry Jacquett demanded that the women return to work, but they laughed at him and refused. Jacquett's boss, realizing that all of the phone service was essentially shut down, approached the leaders of the strike. They said that they would return to work if he promised to restore their biweekly half-day. After a couple minutes of arguing, the boss relented and the women returned to the switchboards. The entire strike and negotiation lasted only ten minutes.

Railroad Directors in Accident on Their Own Line

Several top railroad officials were involved in an accident with another train on their own line in the late morning of March 15, 1880. J.E. Farnum, the president of the West Chester Railroad, and directors Washington Hickman and William Malin were traveling on a special train down the line on a tour. At Forty-eighth Street and Woodland Avenue, their train collided with a passenger train headed in the opposite direction on the same track. The passenger train was coming from Angora. Though both train engines were severely damaged, injuries were minimal. The company executives received only minor cuts and bruises.

The accident was a result of a missed message. The train carrying the directors had telegraphed the Angora station to hold the passenger train until it passed. However, it failed to make sure that the train was still there. Unfortunately for everyone involved, the train was running on time and had already left. The telegraph operator at Angora quickly sent a message back warning of the departure, but by that time the directors' train had also left.

Shark Caught in the Delaware River

By the end of the day on April 30, 1922, Captain Joseph Fletcher of the Wissonoming Yacht Club had the best fishing story on the Delaware River. He did not need to exaggerate either. Fletcher came home that day with a twelve-foot shark. He, in his boat, and other people on the riverbanks had spotted the big fish near Tacony. They were all surprised to find it so far upriver, close to one hundred miles away from the open ocean. Fletcher pursued the shark in his yacht as the people ran alongside on the banks to watch. He finally caught the "man-eating" shark (as it was described in the paper) not with a rod and reel but with a gun. After firing several rounds from the deck of his boat, the shark was dead. It is not known what he did with his bullet-ridden catch. From the descriptions given in the press, it is likely that Fletcher caught a bull shark. Bull sharks can grow up to twelve feet in length and have a tolerance for fresh water. They have occasionally been found in rivers around the world.

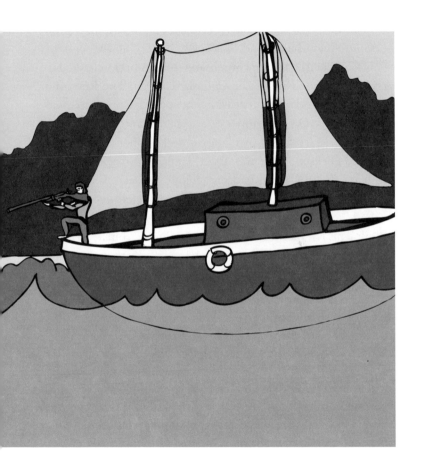

A MIRACLE AT ST. JOHN MARON CHURCH

A miracle was said to have occurred at the St. John Maron Church at Tenth and Ellsworth Streets at the end of December 1904. The church and its members belonged to the Maronite Rite of the Catholic Church. The Reverend Stephen Korkemaz (occasionally spelled Corkemaz) was the pastor. On December 27, a young Protestant woman named Mary Dickson came to seek Father Korkemaz's help. Dickson, who was from Trenton, New Jersey, had heard that the priest had miraculously cured a severe case of rheumatism by praying with the afflicted person. She had hoped that Father Korkemaz could help with her ailment. For months she had been suffering from a "nervous affliction" that had taken away her voice. By that point, she was completely unable to speak.

After communicating her wishes to the priest, presumably through writing, they sat down to pray. Father Korkemaz read parts of the Gospel that dealt with healing miracles, said some prayers and then touched the young woman's throat with a relic of St. Maron. When he was finished, he told her to go home and that her voice would return. Sure enough, after Mary Dickson returned to her home, she was able to speak. A few days later, a friend of Dickson's came to the church to tell the priest that she had been cured. Father Korkemaz insisted that the cure had nothing to do with him personally but was the result of prayer and the intercession of St. Maron.

ALLIGATOR STRIKES IN PHILLY POOL

Bobby Rogers had spent the early months of 1930 in Tampa, Florida, learning to wrestle alligators. According to the *New York Times*, he brought a three-hundred-pound gator to Philadelphia in late August to give demonstrations at an unnamed local pool. Rogers was being assisted in this dangerous sport by his younger brother George. The first day did not go well.

Bobby began the "match" by grappling the alligator's tail. The reptile did not take kindly to the treatment and lunged at his wrist, causing a superficial wound. Bobby quickly decided that it was necessary to tie the reptile's mouth shut. George got hold of the gator's jaws and was holding them shut while Bobby attempted to wrap a rope around them. The angry alligator suddenly lurched free and clamped its teeth down on the lower half of George's left arm. Before Bobby could react, the gator rolled over three times, severing George's arm below the elbow. The *Times* did not record the reactions of the spectators, but we can safely assume that it was a combination of shock and horror. George was rushed to the hospital to save what was left of his arm, and the alligator was put down after the incident.

THE BALLOON HOAX

In the late 1700s, hot air balloons were becoming popular in Europe. The first was flown in France in 1783, and it did not take long for the account of the flight to spread. Soon, hot air balloons were objects of fascination throughout the continent and in America. Though no balloons had yet flown in the United States, it did not stop a mischievous Philadelphian from playing a balloon-related joke on his French friends. The scheming hoaxer sent word to several French newspapers that a Philadelphia man named James Wilcox had taken to the air in a slightly different flying contraption.

The *Journal de Paris* reported that David Rittenhouse and Francis Hopkinson had been experimenting with their own balloon-based flight in Philadelphia. First they filled a cage with animals and attached forty-seven smaller balloons and a rope to it. They floated the cage into the air as a test and pulled it back down with the rope. The men then decided to pay Wilcox to ride in the cage. They let him go up in the air twenty feet and then pulled him back down. The pair haggled with Wilcox over a second attempt, and he finally agreed to have the rope cut for fifty dollars. According to the men's calculations, he could not rise higher than ninety-seven feet. A medical man named Dr. Juane was at the scene in case of an accident. When the rope was cut, the crowd watched Wilcox ascend. He remained calm as he went up, but after about five minutes, a strong wind began to blow. It pushed the balloons in the direction of the Schuylkill River. Wilcox began to worry that he would end up in the water, so he drew his knife and pierced three of the balloons. Though it lowered him a little, he still was not coming down, so he pierced three more. Though Wilcox dropped a little more, he still needed to go lower. In a state of panic, he cut five more balloons—but all on the same side of the cage. It rocked back and forth in the wind. Finally, as it approached the ground, the cage tipped, and Wilcox fell out into a ditch near the river. His only injury was a sprained wrist.

Though the story sounded convincing, the entire event was fabricated. It was believed by many in Paris for weeks, until reporters from the French press asked for more details. Even when no details could be obtained, the hoax was still believed and propagated by those with an interest in aviation until the early twentieth century.

Ten years after the hoax, however, the first real hot air balloon flight in the United States did occur in Philadelphia. French pilot Jean-Pierre Blanchard received a commission from George Washington himself to make the fifteen-mile flight from Philadelphia to New Jersey. The flight, which occurred on January 9, 1793, took Blanchard forty-six minutes. He reached a height of 5,812 feet.

AN OMINOUS DREAM

John Kinsey awoke one morning in 1748 feeling very uneasy. While he was sleeping, he had a dream that his deceased cousin appeared and warned him that he should prepare to "change worlds." Then he heard a loud explosion and fire struck the side of his face. The disturbing dream woke him immediately. After he calmed down and got back to sleep, he had more dreams that carried similar warnings.

At breakfast, Kinsey was still shaken and tired from the night's events. He revealed the details of his dreams to his family. His father, Judge Kinsey, and mother decided to send for some of his friends to help cheer him up. When they arrived later that morning, the friends suggested that they spend the day shooting out in the woods. Kinsey's mother urged him not to take his gun, but her pleas did not dissuade him. He should have listened.

Kinsey and his friends had to first cross the Schuylkill River to get to the forest, so they went to Gray's ferry. The group crossed the river without incident and spent a relaxing day in the woods. When it was time to go home, the friends again loaded themselves onto the ferry. Their rifles rested on the bottom of the boat as they crossed. For some reason that was never determined, Kinsey's gun suddenly discharged. The shot pierced the side of Kinsey's face and entered his brain, and he died instantly. It seems that the warning in his dream had come to pass.

A Ride through a Sewer

On April 28, 1885, workers from the highway department were trying to fix a damaged sewer beneath Willow Street. The passage of freight trains overhead had taken a toll on the walls of the sewer, causing cracks and shifting. Timbers were used to prop up the collapsing wall until further repairs could be made. While the men were working, a heavy rainstorm moved into the city. The rain was so intense that it caused flash flooding. As they hurried to finish their job underground, the workers were unaware of the magnitude of the downpour. Suddenly, they heard a rumbling noise. The workers knew that water was rushing through the sewer system in their direction, so they scrambled to get out. Thirty-year-old James Wright was the last man below the street when the water reached the work area. His co-workers above saw him get pushed away from the ladder and down the sewer tunnel by a wall of water. Wright's screams echoed briefly in the dark tunnel. The workers knew that if Wright somehow survived his journey through the sewer, he would be dumped into the Delaware River. They ran to the waterfront where the drainage pipe let out, which was several blocks away, as fast as they could. As they arrived, they watched Wright emerge from the pipe. The force of the water propelled him fifty feet through the air and out into the river. He was clinging to a board, and his shirt had been ripped from his body. Wright was still conscious and started swimming back to the riverbank. Luckily, a nearby rowboat came to his aid. Wright was badly bruised and was bleeding from small wounds but was otherwise all right. When describing his journey through the sewer, he told the press that "the noise was absolutely frightful, and I was turned over and over again like a scrap of paper blown before a gale of wind."

THE FRANKFORD GHOST

In 1883, Elizabeth Street in Frankford was abuzz with ghostly activity. Two men reported that late one evening they saw a white cloud emerge from a stone quarry where several men had been killed. The pair reported that as the cloud rose, it stretched to a height of twenty feet and turned into the shape of a horrible-looking man. They ran away, but the ghost pursued them until they were too frightened to look behind them again.

The following night, another man walked down the street and reported that he saw a ghost. This time, the ghost appeared as a grotesque man draped in white sheets with blue flames emerging from his eyes. The man said that the ghost was three times the size of a normal man and was wearing a diabolical grin. He immediately fled the vicinity and did not attempt to investigate further.

A third man soon reported seeing the ghost; however, his description was much different from the previous sightings. He claimed that he saw the ghost of a man who had been killed at the stone quarry three months earlier. The ghost looked just as the man had in life except that he was wearing his funeral clothes. After the third sighting, others claimed to see the ghost, but their descriptions varied widely. Shortly thereafter, about a dozen people camped out on Elizabeth Street to try to catch a glimpse of the now notorious neighborhood phantom. At one point during their vigil, members of the group noticed a mysterious white figure in the center of the block, but when they approached the figure, it disappeared. For the next several weeks, other groups assembled to catch a glimpse of the ghost. It was not reported as to how long the apparition continued to appear.

FREAK STORM

The weather was pleasant for most of the day on May 26, 1927. Up until 3:00 p.m., the skies were clear and the sun was shining. Seemingly out of nowhere, menacing clouds blew in out of the southwest. Moments later, there was a tremendous downpour accompanied by strong gusts of wind. The sudden shift in weather spooked the horses that were out on the grounds at the Devon Horse Show. The animals stampeded, charging through booths, tables and tents that were set up for a dog show that was to occur in a few days. The horse show was not the only entertainment venue that fell victim to the storm. The 101 Ranch Wild West Show had a large tent set up on the circus grounds. As the strong winds gusted through, part of the tent collapsed on over one thousand spectators who were seated inside. While the collapse caused numerous superficial wounds, only two people were injured badly enough to be hospitalized. All around the city, trees were uprooted, power lines were knocked down and roads were obstructed. Half an hour after it began, the storm ceased. By 4:00 p.m., the sky was sunny and clear again.

Arrest That Woman...and Her Monkey!

Police Officer Mitchell was walking the beat in the second ward on a warm, mid-August afternoon in 1882 when he came across a woman causing a disturbance. Lydia Brown was staggering about the streets in an intoxicated state. Brown was well known to the police and was described as "the proprietress of a notorious house." In other words, she ran a brothel. Brown was also known for her pet monkey, which had been given to her by some sailors who frequented her establishment. The monkey and Brown were inseparable, so when Officer Mitchell arrested Brown, the monkey came too.

While walking back to the police station, the pair came within sight of a friend of Brown's named Mrs. Little. Little was well known in town, and she prided herself on her toughness and the fact that no one could beat her in a fight. When she saw her friend being taken away by a policeman, she decided to get involved. As they passed by, Little shouted at Officer Mitchell and attacked him. As Mitchell tried to defend himself from the woman and hold onto Brown, the monkey jumped on his head. When he tried to remove it, the animal bit his finger. By this point all three (and the monkey) had fallen to the ground and were rolling around in the street. Mitchell finally subdued Little, stood up and marched Brown and her monkey straight down to

the station and into a jail cell. He immediately turned around, walked back to the scene of the altercation and arrested Mrs. Little, who was still lingering. Little was upset that she had been bested by the officer.

Hero Killed by Runaway Horse

A doctor left his horse and buggy standing in front of his home at 701 Christian Street on the evening of February 12, 1902. While he was inside, a mischievous boy crept up on the horse and whipped it. As a result, the frightened animal charged up the street at full speed. Pedestrians jumped out of the way and shouted warnings to those in the horse's path. An Italian woman and her child were crossing the street at Eighth and Christian. They happened to be right in the path of the runaway horse. Even though the woman saw the horse, she became confused and froze in her tracks. It was only a matter of seconds before the two would be run down.

Luckily for the woman, a thirty-three-year-old man named Samuel Brown was watching the events unfold from a passing streetcar. Brown jumped out of the streetcar and darted toward the pair. He reached them just in time to push them out of the way. Unfortunately, Brown was unable to move out of the way himself and was knocked to the ground by the horse. The animal trampled Brown and pulled one of the wheels of the buggy over his head. Bystanders rushed to his aid and carried him to a nearby house. Doctors arrived quickly, but too much damage had been done. Brown was unconscious most of the time but managed to wake up long enough to ask if the woman and child were all right. When he knew that they were safe, he lapsed into unconsciousness again. He was taken to Pennsylvania Hospital but died about half an hour later from his wounds.

The Witch of Ridley Creek

The only official witch trial to be held in the state of Pennsylvania occurred in Philadelphia in 1684 before none other than the great William Penn. Witches were a cause of great concern in the early days of the settlement of the New World. Witchcraft-related relics dating from the 1600s were even unearthed during the construction of the Philadelphia Airport. The Salem Witch Trials were the most notorious of the witchcraft prosecutions of the colonists, and while the motives for the accusations were similar in Philadelphia, the outcome was drastically different.

Swedish immigrants had settled the best farmlands along the Delaware River prior to King Charles II granting the land, later named Pennsylvania, to William Penn. The English settlers who arrived after Penn's grant had a tougher time finding arable lands for farming and grazing cattle. This resulted in much enmity between the English and Swedish settlers. Margaret Mattson and her husband were two of the successful Swedish settlers who inspired jealousy in their English neighbors. It is against this backdrop that Margaret Mattson and another woman were charged with witchcraft. The charges against the second woman were dismissed, and Mattson proceeded to trial in front of William Penn, an attorney general and twelve jurors.

Three men testified that they heard that Mattson had bewitched cows, and another man claimed that she had conjured a spirit and frightened her daughter-in-law. Mattson vehemently denied the accusations and correctly pointed out that most of the testimony against her was hearsay. At one point during the trial, William Penn asked, "Art thou a witch? Hast thou ridden through the air on a broomstick?" Because Mattson did not speak English well, she misunderstood and answered yes. William Penn pointed out that flying through the air on a broomstick was not a crime. However, Mattson was found guilty "for having the common fame of being a witch but not guilty in the manner and form of that which she was indicted for." Her husband was ordered to pay a $100 fine and guarantee her good conduct for six months. In light of the outcomes of other colonial witch trials and the abhorrence that the Quakers felt toward witchcraft, Mattson was treated rather benignly due to William Penn's good sense and fair judgment.

Watching for Halley's Comet

When Halley's Comet returned in 1910, it caused myriad reactions around the world. Though the comet arrives every seventy-six years, the 1910 visit was unique because of its proximity to the earth and its high level of visibility. In fact, in mid-May of that year, the Earth actually passed through the tail of the comet. This caused considerable worry for many people, especially after it was discovered that the tail contained small amounts of cyanogen gas (cyanide). Even though the gas was not concentrated enough to cause any problems, some feared that the poison would kill off all life on the planet. Unscrupulous salesmen sold "Comet Pills" and other items to "protect" the public from the perceived threat of the comet. There were certainly enough people in Philadelphia who believed that the world would soon end to fill the revival services of the Reverend Abraham Lincoln Johnson. He warned his fear-filled gatherings that the comet heralded the end of days. Others feared that the celestial visitor would somehow cause outbreaks of influenza or other diseases or even cause earthquakes and incite wars.

Though some people were concerned about comet-related disaster, many more awaited the comet with intense curiosity. Comet mania swept the United States as people planned special events around their once-in-a-lifetime chance. In fact, the surprise appearance of another comet in January of that year, the Great Daylight Comet, heightened people's anticipation. The Great Daylight Comet was actually brighter than Halley's and could be seen, as one might guess, during the day. In May, Dr. Charles Doolittle accepted the invitation of the Philadelphia Aeronautical Recreation Society to get a closer look at Halley's Comet than anyone else in the city. The society offered to take Doolittle, who was affiliated with the Flower Observatory of the University of Pennsylvania, high into the air in a hot air balloon for a better view. Also on the flight were Dr. Thomas Eldridge, Dr. George Simmermann and Detective A.L. Millard. The group took off from Philadelphia at 6:00 p.m. on May 20. Though the balloon succeeded in reaching a height of 6,500 feet, the observers were unable to see the comet. Very high and dense clouds had moved into the area and blocked the view. Two nights later, observers on the ground had the same problem while trying to view the comet. They did, however, get to witness a lunar eclipse.

By the time that the comet had passed, many were disappointed that they did not have a better view (and some were relieved that the world did not end). In general, observers in the southern hemisphere fared much better. When the comet returned in 1986, almost everyone was disappointed because it was barely visible. It is thought that the next approach of Halley's Comet will be much more visible—if you can stick around until 2061, that is.

NOTHING STARTS THE DAY LIKE A MAD DOG

It began with cries of "Mad dog!" Over one hundred people were crowded into the intersection of Fifth and Market Streets in the midst of their daily routine on the morning of October 30, 1888. After the cry went out, those people were all running and screaming as a scrawny dog, foaming at the mouth, ran down Fifth Street toward the crowd. Men and women scrambled out of the way. Spooked horses ran off through the crowd, pulling wagons with them. One man holding horseshoes screamed for help as the dog ran between his legs and lunged at a streetcar railing. Calls went out to policemen to kill the animal. One small man emerged from the crowd and boasted that he would kill the dog, but minutes later, he climbed up to the top of a lamp post to escape it. A policeman named Wagner arrived on the scene, drew his revolver and fired two shots at the dog. Both struck the ground around the enraged animal. The dog continued to chase the bystanders, and the policeman fired two more rounds. Again, both of them struck the ground. People continued to run around the street screaming. Wagner fired his last two shots. You can probably guess what happened. As the bullets sunk into the ground, the mad dog paused to scratch itself. Another policeman took this opportunity to run up behind the dog and strike it with a blackjack. It fell dead to the ground, and the excitement was over.

THE MAN WHO WORRIED HIMSELF TO DEATH

In 1885, it was reported that a Philadelphia man had starved himself to death worrying about being bewitched. George W. Kelpin was a professional painter who had been contracted to do work on an addition to the Girard House in Philadelphia. Kelpin needed to borrow money in order to complete the work, and he received a loan from a wealthy man named Samuel Love.

After the job was finished, Kelpin showed Love a bag he kept in his pocket and told Love that the bag had magical powers that kept him safe from being bewitched. Love told Kelpin that this was nonsense and convinced him to rip up the bag and throw it away. Soon after, Kelpin took to his bed sick, and when Love went to visit him, he accused Love of bewitching him. Kelpin's wife and twenty-year-old son also firmly believed that Kelpin had been bewitched.

Love called in a "voodoo doctress" to help cure the allegedly bewitched Kelpin. An African American woman named Sarah Williams from Camden, who was reputed to be a voodoo practitioner, went to the Kelpin home to cure him of his bewitchment. Williams advised Kelpin's wife to place horseshoes under his bed, tie a raw mackerel around each of Kelpin's feet and tie numerous poultices made from raw onions around Kelpin's head. Williams also advised Kelpin to take various medicines and powders to cure his bewitchment.

Believing that the voodoo cures were ridiculous, Love hired a medical doctor to try to cure Kelpin. The medical doctor went to the house and informed Kelpin that dead mackerel and onions could not help him because he was not bewitched. The doctor ordered Kelpin's wife to remove the fish and onions and prescribed medicine to treat Kelpin's nerves. Kelpin refused to follow the doctor's advice and did not take the medicine, and the doctor subsequently discontinued treating him.

A friend of Kelpin's named Edward Watts tried to nurse him back to health during the last two to three months of his life. However, Watts could not cure him of his mistaken beliefs. Watts reported that he refused to eat for the last three weeks prior to his death.

WAS IT A METEOR, A WEATHER BALLOON OR A FLYING SAUCER?

In the years after World War II, the U.S. military took an interest in the phenomena of unidentified flying objects. From 1952 until 1970, the U.S. Air Force conducted an intelligence-gathering operation known as Project Blue Book in an attempt to learn the truth about UFOs. The public became obsessed with "flying saucers" in the postwar years, and the government needed to be sure that there was no national security threat. During Project Blue Book, the air force investigated thousands of UFO sightings from all over the country. Most, though not all, of the cases were eventually dismissed as misidentifications of aircraft or natural occurrences.

One of the cases in the Blue Book files actually predates the operation and was investigated by the FBI. The files were later obtained by the air force. It involves an incident in Philadelphia in August 1947. Several witnesses reported seeing a strange object move through the sky. One of the people who saw it was a retired police officer. He and his wife were sitting on the front steps of his house in the northeastern part of the city at about 10:45 p.m. on August 6. The man looked up and saw an object that he said was shaped like a giant firecracker with a fiery tail that stretched for one hundred feet. The object seemed to be headed south and passed in a few seconds. The man did not believe that it was a meteorite because the object did not appear to lose altitude.

The strange object was also seen by two women and a former pilot from the U.S. Army Air Corps in another part of the city around the same time. The two women were also on the front steps of a house when they saw a fast-moving "bright white" object travel from north to south across the sky. As it passed, one of the women heard a hissing sound. The object left a trail of smoke behind. The former pilot was also sitting on his front steps with his family. His house faced east, and he said that a bluish-white flaming object moved from the northeast to the southwest. Given his background, the former pilot was able to estimate the object's altitude at somewhere between one thousand and three thousand feet. It seemed to be moving at a speed between four hundred and five hundred miles per hour. The man also noticed the hissing sound and the fact that the object did not seem to be losing any altitude in its rapid journey across the night sky. He did not think the object was a man-made aircraft.

Ultimately, the analysts at Project Blue Book decided that this particular UFO fit the description of a slow-moving meteor, despite the fact that it did not appear to descend. A few years later, Blue Book's investigators received another report from Philadelphia. On August 22, 1954, over twenty people saw a mysterious round object in the sky over the northern part of the city. The UFO was silver in color and surrounded by a blue halo of light. When clouds passed in front of the object, the blue light appeared to turn pink. It seemed to hover in the same spot for nearly twenty-five minutes until it "faded" out of sight. The *Philadelphia Inquirer* reported the following day that a total of five UFOs had been sighted that night in eastern Pennsylvania and New Jersey. The paper claimed that it received thousands of calls from witnesses. Several pilots also reported seeing the UFOs. Blue Book ultimately dismissed the sightings, however, because several military observers believed that the objects might be high-altitude weather balloons. The slow movements of the balloons made them appear to hover in one location while they were actually slowly moving farther and farther away from the observers. Skeptics of the government's report claimed that they were too quick to dismiss the case based on an educated guess.

CIRCUS ACCIDENTS

The dangerous nature of many circus acts is what entices audiences to watch. Though the performers may make their routines seem effortless, the slightest miscalculation or mistake could result in injury or death. Given the number of performances that circuses used to put on in a year, accidents were bound to happen occasionally. Several of those accidents occurred in Philadelphia.

A lion tamer for O'Brien's Circus named Joseph Whittle was brutally mauled by one of the animals he was training in April 1872. Whittle was apparently attempting to stick his head in a lion's mouth when the animal clamped down its jaws. Whittle whipped the lion to get it to release him, and it did. Though his wounds were only minor, Whittle angrily continued whipping the big cat. Finally, the lion had enough and pounced on his trainer, viciously tearing at his flesh and crushing his bones. An assistant was finally able to drive the lion off with an iron rod and drag the dying Whittle out of the cage. The press was sympathetic to the lion when reporting the tragedy.

The *Philadelphia Telegraph* reported a tragic accident at a flying trapeze act in April 1880. The Davene family performed a trapeze act in which the mother hung by her feet while holding the ropes of a smaller trapeze from which her husband hung, also by his feet. Their daughter Lucy would swing from another trapeze, fifty feet away, and perform a somersault in the air before catching her father's hands. A rope safety net was stretched below the area where the catch was to take place as a precaution. At a performance on April 15, something went horribly wrong. When Lucy made her initial leap onto the trapeze, she somehow struck her head on the platform. The girl then fell the entire way to the ground because there was no safety net in that area. Three doctors who were in the audience rushed down to help. Lucy was unconscious and bleeding profusely from the back of her head. The paper reported that the injuries were not thought to be fatal, though it described the girl as vomiting blood and possibly suffering spinal damage. Surprisingly, Lucy recovered quickly and was able to perform again within the year.

Fifty-five-year-old Robert White, an employee of Adam Forepaugh's Circus, was killed by an elephant on October 11, 1885. The large elephant was named Empress and actually belonged to O'Brien's Circus. However, it was being housed at the winter quarters of Forepaugh's show. White was the boss painter for the circus, but during winter quarters he had additional jobs. One of those jobs was to bring water to the elephants. When he approached Empress, the massive animal knocked him to the ground and then used her tusk to slam him into the wall of the cage. In the process, the tusk tore into White's abdomen and disemboweled him. He was taken to the hospital, but there was little that could be done.

On May 28, 1932, a performer described as a "wire slider" suffered what proved to be a fatal fall during his act. Julio Olvera's act involved sliding on his head down a one-hundred-foot wire that stretched from a platform to the ground at a forty-five-degree angle. Olvera started his descent that evening as usual and waved to the crowd as he accelerated down the wire. About halfway down, he somehow slipped off the wire and launched through the air, landing on his neck. Clowns rushed out and filled the rings to distract the audience while Olvera was removed and rushed to the hospital. Five days later, he was dead.

Twenty-five-year-old Theodore Simon, a member of the Four American Eagles troupe, died from injuries he suffered after falling from the high wire on New Year's Day 1934. Another member of the group fainted after watching him fall and also fell, breaking his leg. Simon died on January 3 from the internal injuries that he suffered.

They Caught a Ghost

According to the press, a "hideous specter" terrorized the neighborhood around Hirst Street and Gilles Alley for the final three nights of January 1885. The ghost had been seen wandering through the streets among the tenement houses. Witnesses described the specter as being draped in white and moving slowly about. Rumors of the ghost were enough to keep the residents locked indoors out of fear. On the last night of January, which happened to be a Sunday, Mrs. Louisa Cooper was walking home from church. As she reached her residence at 513 Lisbon Street, she realized that something was moving two doors down. She turned and saw the specter slowly "gliding" toward her after emerging from the darkness. The ghost was covered in white from head to toe and made no noise. She said that its face "seemed to shine through as if it were hollow and was lit up from the inside. There were two holes where the eyes should have been." Cooper was extremely frightened by this point. The ghost was moving its head from side to side and appeared to grow taller as it approached her. Finally, she let out a scream and fainted.

Several of the neighborhood men heard the scream and ran to her aid. They saw Mrs. Cooper on the ground and the ghost standing nearby. The men began to chase the ghost, which ran down into Gilles Alley. During the pursuit, the ghost reached down to pull up the slack on his

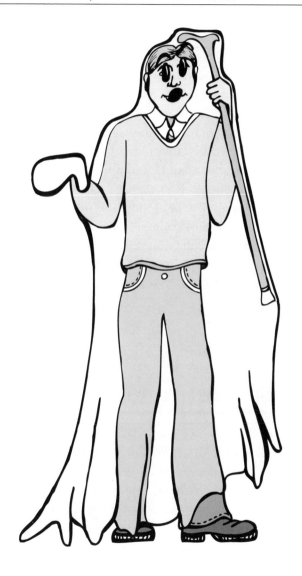

"robe" so that he would not trip. When he did so, it revealed that this particular phantom was wearing pants. The ghost's escape route was blocked by another group of men. The crowd seized the ghost and ripped his costume to shreds. The ghost pleaded, "You needn't choke me, I didn't hurt nobody." They tore off his phosphorescent mask and dragged him out under the gaslight to see who he was. It turned out that he was a waiter who worked at one of the better hotels in the city. Though he gave no explanation as to why he decided to scare everyone, he did explain how he made himself grow taller. He had used a cane to slowly lift the costume above him to give the appearance of growing in height. In the end, the specter had merely been an elaborate practical joke. Mrs. Cooper wasn't laughing.

He Crashed His Wife's Wedding

Austrian immigrant John Powliski was living in Philadelphia with his wife Katarzina in 1901. The couple had married in London nine years earlier, before they moved to the city. Near the end of October, Katarzina left without informing her husband where she was going. Days went by, and she never came home. For three weeks, John searched Philadelphia and neighboring towns in

New Jersey. There was no sign of her. By mid-November, he was informed that his wife was probably in Newark, New Jersey. After receiving the tip, John traveled to Newark, where he happened to run into an old friend. The friend was on his way to a wedding and invited John to come along. He promised him that he would see a lot of old friends.

The pair was running late, but they arrived in the back of the church just as the couple completed their wedding vows. Just then, John spotted his wife—at the altar! Katarzina was the bride, and she had just married Michael Lanko. John began yelling and tried to make his way to the front of the church. Men in the crowd demanded that he leave because they thought he was crazy and had wandered in off the street. When he refused, they forcibly removed him. John went to the police, and warrants were issued for his wife and Lanko. When the police caught up with Lanko, he maintained that he did not know that she was already married. Several others verified that Katarzina told him that she was a widow.

They Tell You Not to Rock the Boat for a Reason

What was meant to be an entertaining afternoon outing turned into tragedy on the Schuylkill River in the spring of 1828. A group of nine young men decided to rent a small sailboat and cross to the western side of the river early in May. They had planned on venturing into the woods there and then later visiting friends. Everything was fine when they set out, but one of the young men started to get rowdy. They were near the middle of the river, across from the United States Arsenal, when the young man decided that he was going to climb the mast. His friends told him that it was a bad idea and made it clear that they did not want him to do it. Ignoring the pleas of his friends, the young man decided to do it anyway. As he climbed the mast, the boat began to rock. When he approached the top, his weight caused the boat to tip in the current and capsize. All nine went into the water, but only four reached the riverbank. The other five young men drowned, their bodies carried off down the river. Though the tragedy was briefly covered in the newspaper, it was not stated if the young man on the mast was among the living or the dead.

The Moon Tree

When astronaut Stuart Roosa circled the moon aboard Apollo 14, he carried with him a unique cargo. Stored in several small containers in his personal kit were over five hundred tree seeds. Roosa was a lifelong lover of the outdoors. Before the Apollo 14 flight in 1971, and before he became an astronaut, Roosa had worked as a smoke jumper. He parachuted out of airplanes for the U.S. Forest Service to help fight forest fires. It was Ed Cliff, chief of the Forest Service in 1971, who suggested that Roosa take the seeds to the moon. The spaceflight would provide the opportunity to see if the exposure to the radiation of space had any effect on the trees. Seeds from five different types of trees were selected for the journey—loblolly pine, redwood, sweet gum, sycamore and Douglas fir.

The seeds survived their journey around the moon but were mixed together when their containers broke on the ground after the flight. Initial attempts to germinate the seeds failed, but a second attempt was successful. The seeds eventually produced close to 450 saplings that were compared to control samples. No differences were detected, and by the mid-1970s, the saplings were scattered around the country and planted. Many were planted in celebration of the bicentennial of the United States. Though NASA lost track of some of the "moon trees" over the years, others were planted in more prominent locations. On

May 6, 1975, the first moon tree was planted by Cub Scouts in Washington Square Park in Philadelphia. The sycamore is still there, surrounded by a small metal fence and marked with a plaque.

PANIC AVERTED BY PATIENT PRIESTS

The 7:30 a.m. Mass on Sunday, September 4, 1921, started out as usual at the Church of the Most Precious Blood. All of the pews were filled with parishioners. The opening prayers and readings went as planned. Around the time that Father William O'Donnell began his homily, however, something out of the ordinary happened. Candles near a statue of the Blessed Virgin somehow caught the surrounding decorations on fire. Both the priest and the congregation noticed the flames immediately as they spread quickly up the wall toward the ceiling, burning anything combustible in their path. Before anyone in the congregation panicked, Father O'Donnell calmly said, "This is a concrete building. There is no possible danger." The congregation remained quietly in the pews. The priest continued, "If two men could step into the hall and get the fire extinguishers, we can easily put this fire out." Two men near the back got up and did just that, while another quietly went to call the fire department. The flames were spreading to a wooden door frame when the men with the extinguishers reached the front of the church. They put the fire out in minutes while the rest of the congregation watched. Once the fire was out, Father O'Donnell continued with Mass. A fire truck arrived a few minutes later only to find that it was not needed.

On May 13, 1928, a similar situation occurred at St. Paul's Roman Catholic Church. Over five hundred people were attending Mass when a candle ignited the altar coverings. A procession of two hundred children was just about to come up the main aisle when the fire started. Just as the congregation began to react to the blaze, Father Edward Lyng signaled the nun in charge of the children to have them begin singing their hymn. The priest began singing as well. As the rest of the congregation joined in, off-duty fireman Frank Vitocalanna and several other men calmly walked up to the altar and extinguished the fire. Mass proceeded as usual.

A GHOST ANSWERS THE PHONE

The Protestant Episcopal City Mission at old St. Paul's Church was receiving some unusual volunteer help in the summer of 1908. A ghost was apparently answering

the phone after hours when the building was locked. Reverend Cresson McHenry and his staff had seen what appeared to be a ghost moving up and down the stairs on various occasions. But when their friends and relatives claimed that they spoke to someone on the phone after the building was allegedly locked, they realized that this ghost was a little more interactive. On one occasion, the wife of one of the staff members called after they had all left the building. A soft-spoken voice told her that her husband would be home in time for dinner. Another time, a friend of McHenry's called in an attempt to reach the minister before he left for the day. His call was answered by a quiet voice that informed him that McHenry "has just left the mission."

On the Fourth of July, McHenry stopped at the mission to retrieve his mail even though the offices were closed. As he entered the gate, he saw a figure on the stairs inside. The ghost slowly drifted up the stairs and disappeared. The minister hurried inside, hoping to solve the mystery. Unfortunately, he could not find the ghost, but he confirmed that all of the doors and windows were locked.

BURIED ALIVE FOR HALLOWEEN

A mysterious businessman from Lancaster calling himself the "Phantom" decided to pull an elaborate stunt in the week before Halloween in 1975. The Phantom was going to be buried alive in Philadelphia for seven days and emerge from the ground on October 31. The man spent the week in a seven-foot-long, three-foot-wide fiberglass coffin. It was buried in a six-foot hole that was excavated in an empty lot downtown. A narrow shaft connected the coffin to a fiberglass tombstone at the surface. Inside the coffin was an emergency air supply, a phone that connected to the surface and a small television set. Food was lowered to the Phantom down the narrow shaft by his wife, who remained on watch. She told reporters that luckily, she had only dropped food on his face once (and it was a salad). Though the entire stunt cost about $5,000 to put together, the Phantom only charged the curious fifty cents each to peek down through the tombstone at him.

A LION ON THE LOOSE

In the early 1880s, Peter Marvine was an animal trainer for J.B. Doris's Inter-Ocean Circus. As one would expect, he cared for, taught and fed the animals when the circus was traveling and when it was camped for the winter. In 1883, the circus had its winter quarters in Frankford. Though practice and preparation were continued all year, the winter break allowed the circus workers a little time to relax without having to perform. Animals and equipment were housed in buildings to provide refuge from the weather. The circus had several buildings on Harrison Street for this purpose. Every day, Marvine would visit the animals, feed them and practice tricks if necessary. But on one cold and mundane January day, Marvine's routine almost turned deadly.

The incident occurred in a room that housed the tropical animals. The fifty-foot room was full of iron and wooden cages, some of which contained lions, tigers and other large cats. Juno was the largest lioness at the circus, and she had recently "adopted" two motherless cubs. The five-year-old lioness was known to be one of the best-behaved animals in the show. At that time, the cubs were in a cage near Juno's so that they could see each other and interact. There was no reason to expect that this would lead to any trouble. When it was time to feed the animals, Peter Marvine stopped at the cage as usual to give the cubs their share of liver. Unfortunately for Marvine, he paused for a moment and decided to pet the cubs. Juno became agitated and roared at the trainer. Marvine moved away from the cubs and slowly walked toward Juno's cage to calm her. Just as it seemed the lion would settle, Marvine tripped and fell against the cage. When his right arm slipped through the bars, Juno pierced his flesh with her claws just above the elbow and trapped his arm inside the cage. Marvine grabbed one of the bars with his left hand to get leverage, but he could not pull himself free. Juno lashed out with her other paw through the bars and struck Marvine in the head and neck. Another circus worker named Donahue witnessed the attack and ran to aid the trainer. He struck at the animal with an iron bar to try to make her release the man, but it only enraged her further. As Juno roared, the other animals became agitated and made so much noise that they could be heard several blocks away. Donohue realized that he needed to get more help and ran from the room. At that point, Juno released Marvine, and he dropped to the ground. His arm and shoulder were shredded, but he managed to crawl a short distance away from the cage.

Moments later, Donahue returned with more men. As they entered the doorway, the men were greeted with a deafening roar and the even more terrifying sound of a cage being ripped apart. Juno had broken free, so they slammed the door and listened from outside. The lion could be heard moving around in the building, and other animals would screech and roar when she approached their cages. Donahue and the other circus men assumed that Marvine had been killed. The tough trainer, however, had crawled his way over the wall and retrieved a heavy iron bar. Despite the pain, he returned to his feet and marched back toward Juno, who was now in a corner. Marvine boldly commanded the lioness to get back into what was left of her cage. This time, Juno complied. When the men outside heard Marvine's voice, they entered the room to find that the situation was under control. Marvine was seriously injured but recovered and eventually regained most of the use of his arm.

Deadly Fire at the Factory

On January 19, 1910, a deadly fire broke out at Joseph Chachkin's shirtwaist factory on Chancellor Street. The blaze started in the elevator shaft near the fourth floor when the electric motor short-circuited. The fire spread quickly and trapped many of the young workers, who were mostly women, on the upper floors. Owner Joseph Chachkin and two of his daughters were also working that day because part of the regular labor force was out on strike. Panic spread among the workers as they desperately tried to escape the smoke and flames.

Bystanders who were watching the fire in the street tried to help. Men stretched out blankets and awnings to catch any of those who jumped to escape the flames. Unfortunately, the smoke that was billowing out of the lower windows blocked the view for those trying to jump from the upper floors. Four of the young women were killed when they jumped to the street below, fracturing limbs and skulls. Some workers were severely injured in the drop, even if their falls were partially broken by the outstretched blankets. One young man broke three of his four limbs. Others suffered from internal injuries and smoke inhalation. One man attempted to descend from a rope, only to fall to his death. Other fleeing workers used ropes, only to slide down so fast that the ropes cut their hands to the bone. For Joseph Chachkin, the day would get even worse. One of his daughters, sixteen-year-old Elizabeth, was burned in the fire and then killed when trying to jump from the building. Another daughter, fourteen-year-old Rebecca, suffered burns, a fractured skull and other internal injuries. She was not expected to survive but lingered on for a brief time. Joseph did survive but was also injured. What makes the fire even more tragic is the fact that the building did have fire escapes, but the general panic and the obscured view prevented their proper use.

The "Cloak Man" of Clifton Heights

A mysterious figure in a black cloak and hood caused a good deal of fright and concern in Clifton Heights in November 1916. The cloak man emerged from the shadows of Walnut Street and other nearby roads to frighten couples as they were out walking in the evenings, though he caused no physical harm. His repeated appearance sent the neighborhood into a panic. One particular incident was detailed in the *Chester Times*. On Saturday, November 23, a young man named Joseph Austin was accompanying a young woman back to her home about 11:00 p.m. The couple was on Walnut Street, approaching the intersection with Fairview Avenue, when the cloak man emerged from the shadows and stood in front of them. The cloak man held his hand in front of Austin's face and mumbled something that was unintelligible. Both Austin and the young woman were gripped with terror, but the cloaked figure did nothing else except turn and run away. The cloak man had apparently appeared to several other couples earlier that same evening.

The young man alerted Police Chief McGowan, who in turn rounded up a posse to help search for the cloak man. A few men thought they spotted him in a nearby orchard, but the mysterious figure escaped before they could get close. They were unable to locate him after that. The following evening, the chief went undercover as a civilian and walked the streets, hoping to catch the cloak man. He had no luck, but the cloak man appeared in a different part of town. This time, the couples that he approached noticed something unusual. Underneath his black cloak, he was wearing women's clothing. His continued appearance caused many people, especially women and children, to avoid walking around after dark. Those who did were usually accompanied by a husband or male companion. Some young men continued to patrol the streets in groups hoping to catch the cloak man and extract their own punishment. This seemed to have some effect, because by the end of November, the cloak man was only spotted at a distance and had stopped approaching people on the street. It does not appear that he was ever caught.

The article in the *Chester Times* cited a similar incident that had occurred "many years ago" in the same area.

Apparently, a man named Stillwagon had been approaching and harassing young girls while dressed in a cloak. He continued for several weeks before he was arrested by Officer J.M. Lungen. It is not known if the two cloak men were somehow connected or if Stillwagon was somehow tied to the "Ghost of Clifton Heights" discussed earlier in this book.

Rattlesnake Joe

An elderly man named Joseph Martin, also called Rattlesnake Joe, caused quite a stir in Philadelphia in May 1882 when he stepped off a train at Broad Street station carrying a tin can in one hand and a rifle in the other. He was in town asking for the address of a prominent druggist. Rattlesnake Joe was an eccentric and highly regarded purveyor of rattlesnake oil, and he was in town to sell his product. His bizarre appearance, long white hair and beard and rumors of his strange lifestyle fueled the aura of eccentricity that surrounded the strange old man.

Rattlesnake Joe hailed from a mountainous area of Cameron County, Pennsylvania, where rattlesnakes lived in abundance. It was reputed that he spent years combing the woods and mountains for the snakes with minimal, if any,

human contact. The old hermit caught the rattlesnakes with a stick, cut off their heads, skinned them and then reduced them to fat by boiling them to make his very profitable oil. Many people believed that the oil could relieve the symptoms of rheumatism and other ailments. It could also be used to grease the parts of small mechanical devices, such as watches.

The profitability of his snake oil fueled the legend of Joe's riches. Whether in Philadelphia or elsewhere, Joe peddled his oil to physicians and superstitious people alike. Allegedly, he had a substantial amount of money at one point in his life, although not everyone believed that he still possessed it. Some rumors asserted that Joe lived as a hermit because decades before his girlfriend had run off with all his money and broken his heart. Some people simply believed that the old man was crazy. After he finished his business in the city, he returned to the mountains to trap more snakes.

"MURDEROUS POLICEMEN"

That was the title of an 1876 *New York Times* article about several Philadelphia police officers who were accused of crimes that violated their oath to serve and protect. The article had come from the *Philadelphia Times* and chronicled the misdeeds of the rogue officers over the previous year and a half. The men profiled were a mix of current and former officers, all of whom were charged with murder.

The first killing occurred on May 29, 1875. Three off-duty officers from the Eighth District were still carrying their firearms when they got into an altercation on Ninth Street. James Mervine, Frank Barclay and John Flowers ran into a man named George Alexander, with whom they had previous disputes. Instead of resolving this incident with their fists, the officers shot Alexander four times at point-blank range. The officers then pushed his body into the street. All three went to trial but claimed that they were drunk and would not have otherwise killed the man. They managed to avoid the death penalty. Mervine and Barclay were each sentenced to nine years in prison. Flowers initially escaped prosecution, but once his name was known in the press, he turned himself in as an accessory to murder.

The next murder occurred on June 27. A former police officer turned neighborhood bully, Jack Hart, was the killer. Known as "Jack of Hearts," Hart killed a stranger named Michael Kerwin at Fifth and Bainbridge Streets. Kerwin had apparently warned Hart not to insult a woman. Hart did not like being told what to do. He stabbed Kerwin, killing him almost instantly. He was also convicted and sentenced to nine years in prison.

Another murder was committed on June 4, 1876. Officer James Platt left a group of friends and acquaintances in

Germantown early that morning. On the way home, he came to believe that one of the men he had previously been with had robbed him. He retrieved his pistol and returned to the group. All of the men fled, with the exception of Robert Craig, the presumed thief. Platt shot him dead. Though he pleaded drunkenness, he was convicted.

The final murder occurred on August 30, 1876. Officer Socrates Keenan bludgeoned the vagrant Francis Quinn on Hagner's Avenue. It is not clear exactly why Keenan attacked him, but it was overheard that he was waiting to ambush the man. Keenan then had Quinn sent to jail, where he died shortly after arrival. Keenan's case was going to trial at the time the article was written. He was later acquitted.

EXPLOSION AT THE MEATPACKING PLANT

A bad accident occurred in the meatpacking factory owned by Jacob Alburger on November 8, 1861. The building was located at the corner of Sixth and Reed Streets. The incident occurred about 11:00 p.m., and there were few employees in the building. A large, two-thousand-pound iron tank that was used for boiling bones suddenly exploded. The top portion of the tank fired into the air like a rocket, bursting through the roof and traveling six hundred feet through the air until it plummeted into the yard of William Tiller on Fifth Street. The tank tore though a brick wall and a fence on Tiller's property before coming to rest in the outhouse. Luckily, no one outside the factory was injured. The same could not be said of the three employees who were working near the tank at that late hour. When the explosion occurred, the hot fat and grease that had built up inside flew everywhere. One of the men, John Brown, avoided injury because he was in a stooping position. Christian Siegal, a butcher, and Jacob Sigmund, the night watchman, were both severely burned by the fat. Many more would have been injured had the accident occurred during the day. Brown, who was an engineer, could not figure out why it happened. He claimed that pressure in the tank had been normal up until the instant that it had exploded.

A Pre-Halloween Prank

Halloween, and the entire month of October, has long been a time when people love to scare themselves and think about ghosts and goblins. It has also traditionally been a time for mischief and pranks (which often get out of hand). In early October 1948, some person or persons decided to get a head start on the Halloween season and pull a prank on a north Philadelphia neighborhood. On the morning of October 8, people living near Twenty-seventh and Arizona Streets awoke to find a surprise on their sidewalk. Resting in a long, open coffin was a human skeleton. A few residents who approached the coffin, upon realizing its contents, ran away. Others saw the skeleton and screamed, alerting the rest of the neighborhood to its presence. One thing that they all agreed on was that none of them was going to touch it or move it. Eventually, the police were called to retrieve the unwanted anatomical specimen. The coffin and its contents were taken to the police station. Nobody had seen who had placed it on the sidewalk. Police speculated that the skeleton was left by either a member of a secret society or a medical student playing a joke.

BATTLE OF THE ELEPHANTS

Four elephants on a circus train caused their handlers quite a bit of trouble as they traveled from Harrisburg to Philadelphia in November 1902. The handlers thought that the animals were becoming a bit restless as they were loaded on the train, so they chained them in different corners of the large car. As the train picked up speed, the elephants became so agitated that they broke free from the chains and restraints.

Immediately upon freeing themselves, the elephants began to fight one another. They trumpeted loudly and charged into one another in the boxcar. Every impact shook the walls of the car. The animals' handlers scurried out of the way and told the engineer to get to Philadelphia as fast as possible. Little could be done while the train was moving.

The elephants continued fighting as the train pulled into Fair Hill Junction. The four handlers, as well as two policeman and numerous railroad men with poles and clubs, approached the car. The animals were slamming one another into the now weakening wooden walls. Suddenly, the boards at the back of the car were knocked out by the struggling giants. A large crowd had gathered because of the noise, and the handlers feared that the elephants might charge out into the mass of people. They hurried to the opening to separate the animals and keep them away from the crowd. Eventually, they were isolated and calmed by the handlers, but not without a lengthy struggle. No one sustained any serious injuries.

HE LOST PART OF HIS SKULL

F. Marion Davis worked as a heater at the rolling mill of the Philadelphia Iron and Steel Company on North Delaware Avenue. When he reported for his shift on

June 29, 1878, he had no way of knowing that his life was about to dramatically change. Like many other millworkers, he labored around dangerous machines most of the time. Accidents, while not uncommon, were still shocking. While he was working that day, a U-shaped clamp on a nearby fly wheel broke free. The fourteen-pound iron clamp launched across the room like a bullet, and Davis was in its path. The curved end of the clamp slammed into his forehead, causing multiple fractures in his skull. As it pushed through, the clamp drove a piece of his skull through and out of his head. Part of his brain was ejected, and the blood vessels in his head ruptured. Davis also suffered damage to his sinuses, jaws and teeth.

Davis was carried back to his home, where Dr. I.G. Young examined him. Dr. Young felt that the injuries would prove fatal but called in Dr. D.H. Agnew, a surgeon, for a second opinion. Agnew, who was also a professor at the University of Pennsylvania, agreed with Young's conclusion. The doctors still attempted to do everything that they could to save his life. After three days, Davis was still clinging to life, but the doctors did not hold out hope for recovery. Despite the traumatic damage, Davis continued to survive. When he lived into a fifth week, the doctors changed their minds, though Davis was still not out of the woods. After nine weeks, the missing parts of his skull were covered by soft tissue. A month and a half after that, the doctors reported that some boney tissue had grown back, though "the pulsations of his brain" were still visible. Though Davis ultimately made an almost complete recovery physically, he suffered some mental deterioration. Still, he fared much better than doctors had expected.

For more than a decade after the accident, Davis was entangled in lawsuits trying to secure compensation for his injury. After suing the Philadelphia Iron and Steel Company over the injuries and hazardous conditions, Davis was awarded $20,000. The company appealed, of course, and found a more sympathetic judge the second time around. Though Judge Biddle still held the company partially responsible, he reduced the payment to $10,000 because human errors made by other employees may have contributed to the accident. In 1886, the company appealed again, brazenly claiming that it held no responsibility because the engineer whom it hired to inspect the equipment failed to properly perform his job. This time, the judge agreed with the company and decided that it did not owe Davis any compensation. Davis was informed that if he wanted payment for the accident, he would have to bring a lawsuit against his former co-worker. It is not clear if Davis decided to pursue any further legal action.

THEY BLEW THEIR OWN COVER

An explosion tore apart a boardinghouse at 735 Wood Street on the evening of November 11, 1903. Thirty-one-year-old James Patton, who was closest to the source of the blast, was severely burned. Ten other people ran out into the street to escape the fire. The explosion occurred in a room that had been rented out only five weeks earlier. When police and firemen arrived on the scene, they discovered the cause of the disaster. Patton and six other men had been experimenting with dynamite. Why would they be fooling around with dynamite in an apartment, you might ask? The men were part of a gang of safe burglars. When police searched the house they found revolvers, skeleton keys, fuses and guncotton. In James Patton's pockets were maps of Pennsylvania and surrounding states with all the post offices marked. Some of those post offices had recently been robbed, and they were marked with checks on the maps. Needless to say, the men (except Patton) were arrested. Patton was transported to the hospital to recover from his burns before facing charges.

HEY, MR. TAMBOURINE MAN— DON'T COME TO PHILLY

On August 23, 1899, the *North American* ran a very brief article entitled "Beating a Tambourine Is Now a Crime in Philadelphia." Yes, the City of Brotherly Love decided that it did not like to hear anyone playing tambourines, provided that they were playing them with religious intent. (As if you could tell by the sound.) The same held true for drums. Luckily, singing was still permitted, as was playing brass instruments for money. The real intent of the law seemed to be to eliminate the Salvation Army Bands that worked the streets of the city. The article pointed out that several members of the group had already been arrested, and the writer did not hide his contempt for the organization. So much for William Penn's celebrated tradition of religious tolerance.

GHOSTLY SHADOWS

Mrs. Susan Wheeler and her family lived in Frog Hollow in the neighborhood of Roxborough. In May 1896, her family began to see strange shadowy apparitions moving and dancing about her home on the walls. They seemed to appear every night, and the Wheelers thought that they were being haunted. As word spread, neighbors gathered to watch the strange shadowy specters move about the walls. Eventually, hundreds came to witness the ghosts. After several nights of careful observation, some witnesses came to a startling realization. The strange shadows were, in actuality, just shadows. This shocking revelation came when a careful observer thought to look outside. Two arc lamps in the distance caused the shadows of pedestrians who were walking on Ridge Avenue, which was over one hundred yards away, to be projected onto the walls.

OLD COINS DISCOVERED

In January 1872, some boys made a rather fortunate discovery in a cellar that was being excavated in an unnamed Philadelphia neighborhood. The *New York Times* reported that a stash of old coins wrapped in parchment was discovered beneath an old hearth stone. The stone was ten feet below street level and probably part of an early colonial home. At first, the boys did not think that the coins were real and believed them to be made out of brass. They tossed them around and gave thirty of them to a man driving a cart. Eventually, they took a few of the coins to a jeweler, who ascertained their value. Based on what he saw and what the boys told him about the other coins, he estimated their value at $25,000. Once the boys knew the value of the coins, they would not show them to anyone, except a few reporters.

Many coins dated from the time of the first settlers and before. The oldest coin, of undetermined origin, dated to 1603. Several British coins bore the image of King Charles II. Some of the coins were shaved or split into halves and quarters, which was once a method for making change. Another coin from 1720 was imprinted with a Maltese cross and bore the inscription "*In hoc signo vinces*." The newest coin that the boys allowed anyone to inspect was of French origin and dated to 1747. The total number of coins that was discovered is unknown, but it was believed to be a sizeable number. Their ultimate fate is also unknown, but most were probably sold to collectors at a later date.

SAM SCOTT—PHILLY'S FAMOUS JUMPER AND DIVER

Samuel Scott of Philadelphia made a name for himself as a daredevil in the 1830s and 1840s. His leaping and diving abilities, combined with his willingness to take risks, made him popular among audiences looking for excitement. Scott first began jumping in the navy, where he was known to dive off the masts of ships. His jumps and associated theatrics always entertained his fellow sailors, and he soon realized that people were willing to pay to see him risk his life. Scott always jumped into water, often from bridges, ships, cliffs or other high structures. Audiences who gathered to watch would be asked to put money in his hat after his performances. His jumps brought in enough income that he decided to turn his act into a career. Soon he traveled up and down the East Coast and even made a dangerous jump from Niagara Falls. As time went on, he added more tricks to his act to keep the onlookers interested, even performing acrobatics with a noose around his neck. By 1838, he had raised enough money to take his show to England, where he hoped to bring in even larger profits. It was not to be, however. Initially, he entertained spectators there by jumping off the masts of ships, but the crowds would be broken up by police. He then applied for permission to jump off bridges. In early January 1841, Scott was performing at the Waterloo Bridge in London when he accidentally hanged himself with a noose that he was using in his act. Part of his act was a mock execution that he had practiced many times. Scott used a carefully adjusted noose with a slipknot to make it appear as if he had been hung from the supports of the bridge. The day of the accident, he had already successfully performed the trick twice. When he attempted it for a third performance, the rope slipped lower than he had intended. The audience looked on, not realizing that there was a problem until it was too late. Bystanders unsuccessfully attempted to revive him after he was lowered from the bridge. He was only twenty-eight years old.

Panic on the Ferry

Chaos erupted on the ferryboat *Columbia* as it crossed the Delaware River from Camden to Philadelphia on January 6, 1890. The ferry was extremely crowded that day. It was also transporting a carriage and its accompanying team of horses, as well as several steers that had recently been brought in from the West. Mrs. Beulah Canfield, Miss Gertrude Browning and Miss Wright were seated inside the carriage so that they could depart immediately after the crossing was complete. Everything was going as usual until the ferry made it about halfway across the river. Without warning, the steers that were in proximity to the carriage began to attack the horses. The frightened animals charged forward on the deck, dragging the carriage with them. Passengers on the boat scrambled to escape the stampeding animals. They dove toward the side rails, stepping on others in the process. The horses did not stop when they reached the end of the deck and plowed right through the railing. The three women on the carriage jumped off just before the horses pulled it into the river. The weight of the vehicle was too much for the animals, and the entire team of horses drowned. The value of the horses and carriage was estimated at $3,000. Many of the passengers were bruised and battered, but no one was seriously injured.

A PLANE CRASH AND A HEROIC STEWARDESS

A routine flight ended in a fiery crash at the Philadelphia International Airport on January 14, 1951. It was almost 2:15 p.m. when the National Airlines DC4 airplane from Newark, New Jersey, was coming in for a landing. The sky was overcast, and a light snow was falling. More importantly, ice and snow had slowly been building up on the runway. As the four-engine plane came in, things seemed to initially go as planned. However, the plane hit the ice on the runway and was unable to slow down. It skidded off the end, narrowly missing an airport guard in his car. As the plane tore through a fence at the end of the runway, its left wing was knocked off on a concrete embedded floodlight. Gasoline sprayed out of the plane onto the ground and everything else around it. The plane finally rolled into a ditch and stopped. Fifteen seconds later, the fire began.

Marine Private Richard Benedict jumped clear of the plane through an open door but returned to the wreckage a moment later to help a woman and her child escape. One woman jumped out of a shattered window with her coat on fire. She quickly discarded it and ran free. The pilot and flight crew managed to climb out of the shattered cockpit and make their way to safety.

Stewardess Mary Francis Housley calmly and quickly led ten passengers to safety at the door of the plane. The ten-foot-high flames crept closer and closer to the remaining passengers. Instead of saving herself, Housley stayed inside and continued to direct people to the door. While she struggled to get the last passengers out, flames blocked the escape route. Housley never reemerged. Seven of the twenty-eight people on board were killed, including Housley. All were women and children. The survivors had minor cuts and burns but no serious injuries. Housley was posthumously awarded a medal by the Carnegie Hero Fund for her bravery.

HALLOWEEN CANDY SCARES

For children, Halloween is supposed to be a time for fun, spooky stories and, of course, candy. However, in recent decades there has been much concern for parents and police over the possibility that some demented individual might tamper with the treats or even poison them. This fear intensified as neighborhoods lost their "community" feel and because people often know fewer of their neighbors than in years past. Every fall, hospitals offer to X-ray treats to check for hidden razor blades and pins. Authorities caution parents to carefully inspect their children's candy before it is eaten. In the days after Halloween, there are often reports of

families discovering some kind of potentially harmful treat. What many do not realize, though, is that the vast majority of such reports turn out to be false after closer investigation, and in reality, there have been very few actual poisoning attempts by strangers. Most often they turn out to be a hoax or a prank, often perpetrated by children themselves.

Philadelphia experienced quite a few reports of dangerous Halloween treats in the 1960s. This is earlier than reports common in many other areas of the country, which tended to occur in the 1970s and 1980s. But the celebration of Halloween was almost exclusively focused on children by that time, so it is natural that societal fears would manifest themselves in such a way, especially in an urban area.

One newspaper article from 1964 only briefly mentioned that police were looking for the source of a can of rat poison that was apparently given to a little girl. It was discovered in her trick-or-treat bag by her mother. The following year, there were reports that police were looking for a person who had given "medicinal capsules" to several young children. There was no follow-up information for either story.

Pills were allegedly handed out to children in several Philadelphia and Camden neighborhoods in 1966. One twelve-year-old found four red pills in his bag. Another child found an inch-long pill that said "Do Not Eat." A nine-year-old boy came home from walking up and down Simpson Street and dumped his candy out on the table. His father noticed two white pills mixed in with the candy. He took them to a pharmacist, who confirmed that they were medicine. Another seven-year-old girl in the neighborhood had started to eat one of the pills but was stopped in time by her sixteen-year-old brother. According to at least one news report, police began to patrol the neighborhood and inspect bags. They supposedly found "numerous" pills. In the northeast part of the city, one girl came home with an entire pillbox full of tranquilizers. Her mother took the pills to a local drugstore to have them identified. A pharmacist said that there were enough tranquilizers to have killed the girl. Police went door to door in the neighborhood to find the culprit but turned up nothing. The girl also reported that several teenagers had intentionally bumped into her and may have dropped something into her bag.

One particular hoax received a lot of coverage in 1969. Fifty-two-year-old Jack Thomas, an unemployed father of three, was accused of placing a razor blade into an apple that he had given to an eight-year-old girl who lived in his housing complex. When the girl showed the apple to her parents after a night of trick-or-treating, they called police and Thomas was arrested. He was taken before a magistrate, who set his bail at $10,000 and said, "There should be a whipping post for people like you." Strangers began calling his house, threatening to burn it down. Others threatened to beat him up when he was released from jail. Luckily for Thomas, a security guard at the housing complex named Matthew Glelochi was suspicious of the girl's story. Thomas, often called "Uncle Jack" by his neighbors, was a well-liked member of the community. Glelochi had seen the young girl hanging out with a thirteen-year-old girl and acting suspiciously, so he questioned them. When their stories did not add up, the police took another look. The girls then admitted that the incident was a hoax and that they had placed the razor in the apple themselves. "Uncle Jack" Thomas was released from jail and was not bitter about the incident (though some of his neighbors now jokingly called him Apple Jack). He did not want the girls to be severely punished and only wanted them to understand the seriousness of such a prank. Six other reports of razors and pins in candy came in that year as well. All of them turned out to be false.

Numerous other reports came in over the following years, and as one might expect, the vast majority turned out to be false alarms. In 1973, one boy in Philadelphia received pills in his bag. Police traced the medicine back to the house of a senile old woman, who had put the pills in the bag accidentally. Almost a decade later, in 1982, papers carried a report of a twelve-year-old boy who contacted police and told them that he had found a razor blade in a candy bar. After more questioning, the boy broke down and admitted that the incident was a hoax. He was then charged with filing a false police report.

Despite the fact that most reports of tainted treats are false, it still pays to be cautious and inspect the candy that trick-or-treaters bring home. Occasionally things work in reverse, and an urban legend can inspire real-life events.

"Sixty Hobos Attack One Man"

That was the dramatic title for an article that appeared in the *North American* on November 20, 1897. The "one man" was a police officer identified only by the last name of Goodyear. He had been walking near Woodland Cemetery and the local almshouse in West Philadelphia on the previous morning when he heard a commotion. It seemed to be coming from inside the cemetery walls. Goodyear looked over the wall and found "sixty of the most villainous-looking hobos" crowded against it on the other side. Twelve of the hobos were beating a young man who looked to be about eighteen years old. Goodyear vaulted over the cemetery wall and landed right in the middle of the men. One hobo, who went by the name of Dixie Van Dyke, drew his knife and went after the officer. At that point, Superintendent Lawrence of the nearby almshouse noticed the fight and called police. As the hobos moved in on Goodyear, he drew his pistol and shot Van Dyke in the leg. Goodyear still received several blows to the head, and his situation did not look good. Luckily for him, help arrived in minutes. Most of the hobos fled when they saw the additional police, and the ten who remained were arrested. Van Dyke was sent to the hospital for treatment.

DEATH FROM IMAGINARY RABIES

According to a newspaper report, Philadelphia laborer Fredrick Miller died from fright in early 1882. Miller worked in a lumberyard in the city and was apparently bitten by a stray dog one day on the job. Miller had a very nervous personality and was immediately concerned that he had contracted rabies from the bite. His co-workers apparently found his concern humorous and started to tease him by implying that he had symptoms of the disease. For several days, the co-workers would ask him if he felt "mad" yet and torment him in other ways. Miller came to believe that he did, in fact, have rabies and began to act erratically. The worry became so intense that his body began to shut down. It was not long before he had worried himself to death. The newspaper did not say whether he died at work or at home but only that his death was caused by fright. Miller never had rabies.

MISBEHAVING CIRCUS FOLK

As already noted, the circus has a long history in Philadelphia. Though it was usually a source of entertainment, it could occasionally bring trouble. Sometimes the workers attached to the various shows that operated in the area were the cause of the problem. The following accounts are a few of the "press-worthy" incidents that occurred during the height of the circus years.

In early January 1884, two employees of Adam Forepaugh's Circus had a deadly argument. The circus was in its winter quarters at Lehigh Avenue and Edgemont Street. Both men were working in their respective tents. Twenty-three-year-old Barney Mack was tending to the elephants, while twenty-two-year-old Arthur Spence took care of the other animals. The men disliked each other, so when Mack entered Spence's tent to wash himself, trouble began. Spence, who was holding a pitchfork, shouted, "Get out of here. I have told you not to come in here!" Mack replied by saying that he could do whatever he wanted to do. He had barely finished the sentence when Spence clubbed him on the head with the pitchfork. Mack dropped to the ground, unconscious. The blow was so forceful that it fractured his skull. A doctor named Haines was called to treat the wound, and Mack was sent to Episcopal Hospital on the verge of death. Police were informed of the incident, and they arrested Spence at the circus. They held him in custody as they waited for Mack to die so murder charges could officially be issued.

More problems occurred in August 1885 at O'Brien's Circus. The residents of the neighborhood around Broad and Dickenson's Streets were becoming angry with the circus's canvasmen. The circus workers had finally received the back pay that was owed to them, so they celebrated by drinking and carousing in local saloons for days. Numerous incidents were reported to local police, and the circus workers staggered around the streets causing trouble. One worker named Thomas Lee was accused of picking the pocket of a local coachman named Charles Lybrand. "Whiskey" Jim Hurley, also a canvasman, got into trouble while drinking at Pleisch's Saloon. At some point, his intoxicated mind told him that it would be a good idea to steal Mrs. Pleisch's shawl. (Why the big circus worker wanted a woman's shawl is anyone's guess.) Whiskey Jim snatched the shawl, but he did not expect Mrs. Pleisch to grapple him and prevent him from escaping. She managed to hold him in the saloon until a police officer arrived. When Officer Lafferty attempted to take Hurley into custody, the drunken man head-butted him and then kicked him in the groin. Lafferty was not happy. He pulled out his blackjack and struck Hurley on the head above the eye. The canvasman dropped to the floor. He was taken to Pennsylvania Hospital, where it was discovered that the blow had fractured his skull, though the wound was not fatal.

Some circus folk did not even have to wait until they were hired to get into trouble. Acrobat John W. Casselli was negotiating for a position in Adam Forepaugh's Circus when he was arrested for stealing money from a streetcar operator. The crime took place on a Wednesday in late March 1889. A week later, Casselli was arrested and brought before a magistrate. There, he was accused of being a career thief from New York. This time, however, the police were wrong. Several of the acrobat's relatives, who were also circus performers, testified in his defense. His sister, who had just returned from performing in Havana, Cuba, pointed out that her brother had only been in town for two days when he was arrested. It would have been impossible for him to have committed the crime. Casselli was no thief but was a well-respected performer from a large circus family. He was released from custody after the hearing.

A manager for the Hagenbeck-Wallace Circus named A.W. Martin was arrested in an apartment on Market Street on May 31, 1913. Martin had been tracked to that particular Philadelphia street by detectives who had been hired by his wife, who lived in Saratoga, New York. His wife had been trying to find him for some time. They had been married for twenty-two years, but in 1912, he left for business and never returned. Martin had provided no information on his whereabouts and left his wife with no means of financial support. When the apartment was raided, Martin was discovered there with another woman whom he had been claiming was his wife. The other woman's name is not known, and it is unclear whether she knew of the real Mrs. Martin. Though another circus manager posted his bail, Martin still had to answer for abandoning his wife.

A BAD COMMUTE

It was 8:40 a.m. on August 2, 1957, the height of the morning rush hour on the Philadelphia subway system. Edward Caswell was the motorman on a six car Broad Street subway train. The morning run had been progressing as usual until his train approached the Erie Avenue platform. Unbeknownst to him, a short circuit in the motor was about to make that commute one that he would never forget. Without warning, the circuit breaker triggered an electrical explosion, derailing the lead car. Caswell was temporarily blinded by the blast but managed to get the doors open so that he and the passengers could escape. A small fire erupted in the electrical insulation under the car, and the lights on the train went out.

Back in the passenger cars, commuters who were battered by the explosion and derailment struggled to escape through the smoke. Many had been cut by flying glass. Those who could not reach a door, especially in the first three cars, smashed the remaining windows to get out. People groped their way to the platform and made their way to the surface. Smoke poured out of the tunnel, and trails of blood stretched from the derailed cars to the street above. Ten fire trucks arrived on the scene to douse the flames and help the wounded. Over eighty passengers had sustained injuries. Though there had been much screaming and panic, none of the injuries was life threatening. Since the fire was relatively small and contained, the subway cars were still in good enough condition to be towed away. Within an hour, the tracks were clear and the subway was running as normal.

"Ball Lightning" Frightens Woman

Ball lightning is an unusual phenomenon that is little understood. It is not even accepted as a real occurrence by all scientists because of its rarity. Instead of lightning traveling in the usual "bolt" form, the electricity forms a ball that moves erratically. A woman who lived in south Philadelphia in 1960 was sure that she had encountered this unusual form of lightning. Louise Mathews had a frightening experience that summer in her own home. As she was resting on the couch in her living room one day, a red ball of light passed right through her front window and blinds without burning or breaking either. As it moved near her, she felt tingling on the back of her neck and head. The ball sizzled and buzzed as it quickly traveled through the air into her dining room. The ball lightning then exited her home by traveling through another window, which also suffered no damage. The frightened Mrs. Matthews immediately called her husband, who quickly left work to return home. By the time he had arrived, the hair had fallen out of the back of her head where she had felt the tingling. Her hand was also burned where she had felt her head. There were no other witnesses who could help to lend perspective on what had happened.

DON'T RIDE YOUR HORSE IN THE RIVER

One warm day in June 1829, a drover identified only as Mr. Smith decided that he would give his horse a bath. Since bathing large animals is no one's favorite task, Smith came up with an easier way to do it. He would simply ride his horse into the Schuylkill River and let it do the work. The only hesitation that Smith had about his plan was due to the fact that he could not swim. Still, Smith figured that if he stayed in the saddle and did not venture too far out, he would be fine. The man and his horse waded into the moving water from the bank opposite the Arch Street wharf. Smith guided the horse farther into the river than he should have. The horse suddenly jerked when it stepped into a hole in the river bottom. The sudden movement threw Smith from the animal, and he disappeared under the water and did not resurface. Almost one hundred people were watching from the banks and the wharf, but all were too far away to help. Some of the witnesses speculated that the horse may have accidentally kicked Smith in the head while it thrashed about in the water. Eventually, the horse swam back to the riverbank. A search was made for the drover's body, but it was not found that day. It is not known if it was ever recovered.

MAN BRINGS SNAKE TO SYNAGOGUE

On April 27, 1884, a strange and disturbed man named George Sears caused an unusual disruption in a local synagogue. Sears stormed into the meeting place of the New Jerusalem Hebrew Association at Wayne and Lake Streets during services. A newspaper article described Sears as a "formidable fellow in appearance, wearing a huge sombrero, sporting a heavy piratical mustache."

The same article said that he was known to carry pistols and knives. This time he was wielding a different kind of weapon—a live snake! Sears was holding the snake above his head as he made his entrance. This frightened several of the people seated closest to him. One man stood up and approached Sears and, after laying his hand on his shoulder, requested that he sit down and not interrupt the service any further. The snake-wielding man refused, shouting that he was going "to kill every Jew in the place." Sears continued with his theatrics, waving the snake in the faces of women and children and kicking over unoccupied seats and benches. He also broke windows and a bookcase as he made his way toward the rabbi. Sears attempted to put the snake around the rabbi's neck but was unsuccessful. By this time, acquaintances of Sears had arrived at the synagogue and tried to talk him into leaving. They managed to get him outside, where he was soon arrested.

THE VOICE ON THE RADIO

A mysterious voice made life difficult for Philadelphia police officers in September 1945. What was described as a "shrill, treble voice" was singing popular music on the same radio frequency that the police dispatchers were using to communicate with the patrol cars. The voice, which was thought to be female, would come on the air sporadically. On September 4, the deep-voiced police dispatcher began to relay information when the voice broke in singing "It Had to Be You." The dispatcher stopped momentarily and then sounded the siren call that preceded all police messages. He then continued giving instructions. His voice and the song merged into "a series of unintelligible noises." The dispatcher finally stopped speaking, but the song continued.

Similar interruptions continued for at least several days. Police suspected that their system was picking up broadcasts from a distant radio station and did not think it was a prank. However, they warned that if it was a prank, the perpetrators would be "singing a different tune when we're done with them—and it won't be on the radio."

Murderer Escapes the Noose— By Poisoning Himself

Edward Parr was a violent and angry man. In 1879, he murdered his own daughter in a fit of rage. He stabbed her seven times with a shoemaker's knife after she called him a "gray haired son of a bitch." He was quickly convicted for his brutal crime, and on June 9, he was to appear before Judge Elcock for sentencing. Since the time of his arrest, Parr had been belligerent and demonstrated no remorse. He had mentioned to other prisoners and guards that he hoped for a quick execution.

On the way to his appearance in court, Parr told one of the escorting police officers, "I ain't afraid of the fire of 1,000 rifles, but I bet you I won't be hanged." The officer ignored him, knowing that the judge would definitely send him to the gallows. When they arrived, Parr's lawyer informed the judge that his client would not be seeking another trial. The judge then asked if Parr had anything to say before the sentence was handed down. As Parr rose to make one brief statement, a slight trembling could be noticed in his hands. He told the judge that he had not intended to kill his daughter until seconds before the crime happened. He also said that he was satisfied with his attorneys and that justice should run its course. As he finished speaking, his voice started to waver and he slumped back into his chair. The judge ordered him to stand back up, and he did so by holding on to the railing. As the judge delivered the final words of his sentence, "and there be hanged by the neck until you are dead," Parr collapsed back into the chair. Everyone assumed that he was overcome by the anguish of receiving a death sentence.

When it came time to exit the room, the bailiff and others could not get Parr to his feet. He seemed completely unable to walk. Suspecting a trick, they lifted the man up as he grasped the railing, but Parr's legs gave out. He dropped to the floor and began convulsing. A pair of police officers then picked him up and carried him to a side room to wait for the arrival of a doctor. A short time later, Drs. Chapman and Andrews arrived and determined that Parr had possibly taken strychnine or a similar poison. The doctors administered morphine to stop the convulsions and sent for a stomach pump, which took over an hour to insert. The coroner arrived around that time and demanded that the doctors keep Parr alive so that he could be hanged for his crime. Chapman and Andrews continued their efforts until 9:00 p.m. before finally conceding that he would not last the night.

It was not clear where Parr had received the poison. Authorities arrested his sons Barney and Edward, thinking that they had provided it. Barney told police that he knew his father had concealed the poison in his clothes but he would never have told police. He also stated that his father had originally intended to murder his daughter's husband on the morning of her death, which is why he was carrying a knife.

It appears that Edward Parr was correct when he told the guard that he would never be hanged. Instead, he spent hours lingering in pain from the deadly poison he consumed. I guess he showed them.

COLLAPSE OF THE REED STREET WHARF

In early July 1856, what was meant to be a night of pleasure and relaxation turned into a night of terror for some residents of the city. The Reed Street Wharf was a favorite destination for locals after sundown during the hot summer nights. Extending two hundred feet into the Delaware River, the wharf was built in three sections, which were connected by small bridges. The water depth at the outmost sections of the pier was twenty-seven feet.

At six o'clock in the evening on July 1, a brace for one of the piers gave way. The wharf did not collapse immediately, however, because ropes also secured the outer sections of the pier. Since the pier was still standing, the crowd that had gathered on that pleasant summer evening believed that the structure was still safe. About an hour and a half later, they discovered that they were mistaken. The outer and center sections of the wharf suddenly crashed into the river. Two hundred persons, mostly women and children, plunged into the water below. The outer section also contained a pair of large shears used for hoisting heavy weight; this crashed down, narrowly missing the mass of bodies trying to stay afloat. As the survivors struggled to get back to the riverbanks, nearby vessels came to their aid. Within a few hours, all those who were still living had been pulled from the water.

Initial reports stated that thirty-five to forty persons drowned, but this was found to be a greatly exaggerated number. Still, ten people, all women and children, did drown in what, in hindsight, could have been an avoidable disaster. Interestingly, earlier that day workers on the pier had a premonition of its collapse. They stopped working and refused to go back onto the structure. Several of the men warned those who had come to the pier for recreation about the danger, but no one listened to them.

HIS BALLOON TRIP DID NOT GO AS PLANNED

On September 25, 1851, S.A. King had planned to launch his hot air balloon from an enclosure at the Zoological Garden in Fairmont. A large crowd had gathered to watch the man's ascent on the very windy day. He was supposed to take off in the early afternoon but had difficulty filling the balloon with enough gas to make the flight possible. It was almost 6:00 p.m. by the time King climbed into the basket. Still, the balloon would not leave the ground. In frustration, King threw out all of the ballasts at once. The balloon only rose a few feet off the ground. It was high enough, however, for the balloon to get out of the enclosure enough to

fall victim to the wind. The basket, with King in it, was slammed against the wall and remained tethered to the ground by only one line.

Spectators ran to steady his basket. Some warned him that the wind was too strong and that he should not try again. Others only encouraged him to make another attempt. King decided to give it one final try. After filling the balloon again, he successfully made it off the ground and out of the enclosure. Unfortunately, his balloon bumped into the nearby Wire Bridge and then became entangled in the telegraph wires. King's basket rocked violently in the wind for several minutes before finally breaking loose. The wind pushed the balloon into the bridge one more time before it began to lose altitude rapidly. It then drifted over the Schuylkill River with the basket just above the surface of the water. As the spectators looked on, the balloon bobbed up and down, dunking King in the water over and over again. At times, he was up to his neck in the river. Though the spectators tried to help, there was little that they could do. Eventually, the balloon limped the entire way across the river and set down on the opposite bank. King was apparently all right and was described as "more frightened than hurt."

A TROLLEY AND FIRE TRUCK COLLIDE

At two o'clock in the afternoon on December 15, 1900, a fire alarm was called in for a blaze at Franklin and Diamond Streets. The firemen who manned the new fire truck "C" at the Second and Norris Streets Station immediately sprang into action. They quickly suited up, climbed onto the truck and sped out of the station. Unfortunately for the firemen, they emerged from the station right in the path of an oncoming trolley car. The large truck was going too fast to stop, and the vehicles collided. The force knocked two firefighters off one side of the truck and into the street. They received minor injuries but survived. Forty-three-year-old Thomas Gwynne was not as lucky. He was hanging on the other side of the truck, right in the path of the trolley. The force of the impact knocked him onto the track and beneath the wheels of the trolley. His body was so badly mangled that the newspaper compared him to wheat being ground between stones in a gristmill. Almost all of his bones were broken. He lingered for a short time in the hospital before he died. After the crash, the remaining firefighters gathered themselves and got back into the truck, which was still drivable. They immediately headed to the fire, but by that time it was under control.

He's Not Dead, He's Just in a Trance!

Dr. Lomis E. Wheat was dead. In fact, he had been dead for the better part of a week when his body was discovered at his Diamond Street home on August 12, 1908. The coroner would later determine that the cause of death was uraemic poisoning. One might wonder why it took so long for the doctor's body to be discovered. In actuality, it didn't. Two friends were with him when he died, but the problem was that they did not believe that he was actually dead. The pair remained with the body for several days.

Why would they think he was still alive, you might ask? Dr. Lomis, Fannie Soult and Florence Buckman were all spiritualists. They regularly channeled spirits for guidance and advice. On this particular occasion, Soult and Buckman believed that the doctor was merely in an extended trance. Apparently, they were oblivious to other signs that he was no longer alive. Dr. Wheat had called the ladies to his house because he felt very ill and had a premonition that something bad was going to happen. He wanted the women to channel their spirit guide, whom they knew as "Dr. Miller." Just as they were beginning their séance, Dr. Wheat fell back in his chair, "frothed" at the mouth and died. The women thought that he had entered a deep trance and decided to wait for further instructions from Dr. Miller as to how they could help Dr. Wheat.

When police came looking for the missing doctor and discovered his body, the women were arrested. Soult claimed that the police did not understand and that she would be able to heal Wheat. The next day, the women were released and no charges were filed. Soult claimed that she had finally communicated with Dr. Miller. The spirit guide advised her to get to Wheat's body, no matter what obstacles stood in the way, so she could bring him back to life. She stated that she would be successful as long as "they have not cut the body of Dr. Wheat into parts." Soult also said, "The world will be startled in a very short time, for it has been preordained that I shall make revelations that have not been made since Christ was on earth. I, like him, have the power to heal and bring the dead back to life." Despite Soult's confidence, bringing Dr. Wheat back from the dead was a little harder than she thought. Though there are no contemporary accounts describing her attempt, if she actually made one, one can be reasonably certain that a man coming back from the dead would have made headlines in at least one newspaper.

Hurricane Hazel Wreaks Havoc

Philadelphia felt the destructive wrath of Hurricane Hazel as it worked its way up the East Coast in 1954.

The powerful storm hit the city about 7:00 p.m. on October 15, with sustained winds as high as eighty miles an hour and gusts as high as ninety-four miles an hour. Fifteen people lost their lives in Pennsylvania as a result of the extreme weather, and major damage was reported throughout the city. Numerous rail lines were shut down because of the number of trees that had fallen onto the tracks. Trolley lines were also affected, so buses had to be used for several days instead. Altogether, 25 percent of the trolleys were out of commission. As one would expect, power was knocked out in much of the area as well. Downed lines blocked intersections, making travel hazardous.

The winds were so strong that a 508-foot oil tanker named the SS *Sheldon Clark* was pushed from its moorings and set adrift from the New Jersey side of the Delaware River. The crew had to hurry and drop anchor until a tugboat came to the rescue. Two of the city's radio stations were also knocked off the air by the hurricane. The transmitting unit of WPEN, located at Seventy-seventh Street in West Philadelphia, was blown down. WIBG lost two of its towers around 6:00 p.m., before the worst of the storm had arrived. A section of the roof of the Standard Theater on South Street collapsed, raining debris on the first fifteen rows of seats and injuring two.

Many people who were on the streets were injured by flying debris. A woman on Market Street was showered in glass when a nearby window shattered. She was taken to the hospital in critical condition. Elsewhere, fifty feet of the roof of the Girard Lumber Company on Sedgley Avenue was blown off and onto houses across the street, damaging their roofs and knocking down a garage. Part of the lumber company's wall also collapsed onto cars parked along the street. A section of the roof of the First Presbyterian Church on Girard Avenue was also torn off. It knocked down power lines and traffic lights. One of the timbers from the roof landed on some parked cars. The Philadelphia County Prison lost two hundred feet of its roof, which ended up on the facility's driveway. At Fifty-first and Delancy Streets in West Philadelphia, a car caught on fire when a live power line fell on top of it.

Intense rain from the hurricane also caused flooding in numerous areas. Eight inches of water remained on Delaware Avenue between Market and Vine when the storm was over. Over seventy-five businesses and homes were flooded in that area alone. The Philadelphia Electric Company built sandbag walls around its facilities to prevent damage from floodwater. Numerous other homes and businesses were damaged throughout the region by a combination of wind and water.

A FRIGHTENING HAUNTING

In July 1890, Mr. and Mrs. David Jordan related their story of a terrifying haunting to the *Philadelphia Inquirer*. David Jordan was a former police officer who, at that time, was working for a trolley company. He and his wife were both well-respected and reputable people. When they told their story to the paper, they were living on Stillman Street. They had moved to that location only a month before to escape the supernatural force that was harassing them in their old home on Croskey Street.

Mrs. Jordan said that from the time they had moved into the Croskey Street home, she felt uneasy. She described the feeling as a "strange sense of dread" that she could not shake off. Though she felt extremely uncomfortable in the house, she did not see anything unusual right away. Then one day, when she walked up to the second floor, she saw what she initially thought was smoke in her sewing room. Nothing seemed to be burning, but the smoke increased in volume as she watched and slowly formed into the shape of a man. Mrs. Jordan was terrified and became even more so when the same vision continued to appear almost every day. When the smoky apparition disappeared, it would leave behind a strong smell of sulphur.

Mrs. Jordan was afraid to tell her husband because she did not know what he would think. For weeks, she lived in fear, wondering if she was actually going crazy. Many nights she sat up, unable to sleep. The situation changed one morning when her daughter asked why she had been calling for her the previous night. The little girl would answer, but there would be no response. That happened to be one of the nights when Mrs. Jordan had actually been sleeping. After her daughter had heard the voice, she decided to confide in her husband and tell him what she had been experiencing. To her surprise, Mr. Jordan confessed that he had also seen similar apparitions and had not told her so she would not worry.

In the days that followed, the haunting became more intense. A strange light would be spotted floating through the house, and lamps would go out without any explanation. Knocking noises could be heard throughout the downstairs and on the front door. One morning when Mrs. Jordan was on her way down the steps to the coal cellar, she felt something pulling on her dress. She tried to ignore it and took a few more steps before an invisible force suddenly pushed her to the ground. Mrs. Jordan attempted to get back on her feet twice, but each time, the invisible attacker drove her to the ground with more force. Finally, she felt paralyzed and was barely able to hear or see. Mr. Jordan came down the steps to help her and said that her face was covered in a phosphorescent light. The light disappeared after he took her upstairs and washed her face with witch hazel.

Several hours later, Mrs. Jordan walked into her bedroom to find her husband lying on the bed, surrounded by the strange light. His pale body was paralyzed, and his tongue protruded from his mouth. After several minutes he could move again, and the couple immediately decided that it was time to leave the house before the supernatural force killed them.

Though their rent was paid in advance, the family began packing up their belongings. However, when they tried to move the furniture, it would not budge. Other men came to help them move, and they could not even lift a mattress. While the men were downstairs trying to find a way to make the furniture move, Mrs. Jordan was knocked to the floor again in one of the bedrooms. Her arm glowed with the strange light once again and turned extremely pale. Hearing her fall, Mr. Jordan raced up the stairs and dragged her out of the room. At that point, he decided that they would leave their remaining belongings and get out immediately.

When the Jordan family moved into their new home, the strange occurrences ceased. The *Philadelphia Inquirer* discovered that a new resident had moved into the haunted house a week before they spoke to the Jordans. They went to Croskey Street to interview the new resident, Mrs. Byrnes, who told them that she had seen nothing unusual in her first week at the house.

THE WORLD WILL END IN 1940!

A press release from the Franklin Institute in Philadelphia on March 31, 1940, caused a brief panic by stating the world would end on April 1. The release indicated that the astronomers at the institute guaranteed that it was no April Fool's joke and the world would come to an end at 3:00 p.m. Eastern Standard Time the very next day. The message went on to say that confirmation of the announcement could be obtained from the director of the Fels Planetarium. The press release might have gone relatively unnoticed if it had not been picked up and broadcast over the air by radio station KYW. The radio announcement was preceded by a show hosted by Jack Benny that discussed the end of the world. Given the source of the press release, many people were genuinely frightened. The station and the Franklin Institute were bombarded with panicked inquiries. The institute announced that it had made no such prediction and sent out no official press release. It was soon discovered that William Castellini, who was involved with public relations at the institute, sent the fake press release to publicize an upcoming lecture that was going to discuss ways in which the world might end. The lecture was scheduled for 3:00 p.m. on April 1. Castellini claimed that he had informed someone at the station about the true nature of the announcement. The institute, like the public, did not find his prank amusing and fired him.

UFO Witnessed by Many

In the early morning hours of October 8, 1975, multiple witnesses watched an unidentified flying object move around in the skies above Philadelphia and Delaware County. Almost fifty people called the police to report a glowing object moving erratically above the sleeping city at about 4:00 a.m. In fact, two of the witnesses were police officers. A sergeant later described what he saw to the press. He said, "It was pretty bright with flares from either side. It seemed to rotate. It would go up and down and crosswise and in a circular motion." The sightings continued for a brief time before the strange lights disappeared. Officials at the Philadelphia International Airport could not explain the mysterious lights but verified that they were probably not from a conventional aircraft. Venus and Jupiter were particularly bright that week in the night sky, but astronomers at the Fels Planetarium of the Franklin Institute doubted that the planets were the source of the phenomenon. The true nature of the UFO was never determined.

A "Witch" Scares a School

The students of L.H. Smith Primary School, located at Fifth Street and Snyder Avenue, were thrown into a panic on February 6, 1896, when a "witch" paid them a visit. How did a witch come to terrorize elementary school students? The trouble actually began two weeks earlier after what most would consider a rather mundane incident. Someone stole a few small coats belonging to some of the young children out of the school's coatroom one afternoon. One of the children had spotted a strange-looking old woman near the school around the time of the theft. It did not take long for the rumor to spread that the woman was a witch and that she had taken the coats. Soon, the witch dominated all conversation among the students. It reached the point that it was distracting the children, so the teachers had to spend class time convincing them that there was no witch and that they were all safe. Despite the assurances of the teachers, the children were keeping a watchful eye out for the villainous old woman.

On February 6, many of the upper grades were empty because of the school's exam schedule. On the building's second floor were three full classes of first-graders and one classroom full of second-graders. One of the first-grade rooms had a view of the coatroom from its door. About 2:30 p.m., it was reported that a little girl looked out the door, turned pale and jumped to her feet. She yelled, "Miss Dunlap! The witch! The witch!" The rest of the children jumped from their seats and ran to the door to get a look at the witch for themselves. When they looked across to the coatroom, they saw an old woman with a strange hat and a broom. The children screamed and ran back into their classroom and through an adjoining door into the next room. At least one child shouted, "She has a gun!" and others kept screaming, "The witch!" Miss Field, who was teaching in the adjoining room, tried to stop the onrush of panicked students, but she was pushed aside. The students in her room panicked as well, as they all attempted to escape the building and the witch. Boys across the hall in Miss Volimer's class jumped out of their seats and joined the stampede in the hallway. Soon, the entire second floor was rushing down the stairwell to get out of the schoolyard.

On the first floor, the teachers had more luck restraining their students when they heard the screaming. They were also able to stop some of the young children from leaving the building and helped to gather those who made it out to the schoolyard. A few students who were extremely frightened slipped away from the school entirely and ran all the way home. After several minutes, the teachers were finally able to calm the students enough that they could go back and determine the identity of the witch. It turned out that the witch was merely an assistant janitor who usually worked after 4:00 p.m. She had decided to start early that day because the older students were not in school and their classrooms were empty. The old woman had entered the coatroom to get her odd-looking hat that she called her "dusting cap." She always wore it while she cleaned, and it happened to be hanging on a hook beneath one of the children's coats. Because of her late start time, the children were not used to seeing her. When the little girl spotted her standing in the coatroom with the strange hat and a broom, it seemed to her that all the rumors were true.

Selected Bibliography

Articles

Atchison Daily Globe. "A Fierce Elephant." October 12, 1885.

Atchison Globe. "A Case of Death from Fright." January 17, 1882.

Boston Courier. "Sam Scott, the American Diver." February 25, 1841.

Boston Daily Advertiser. "The Grave Robbers." December 16, 1882.

———. "The Philadelphia Ghouls." December 14, 1882.

Bradford Era. "7 Die as Airliner Crashes, Burns in Philadelphia." January 15, 1951.

Bulletin. "Harmful Treats Given to Youngsters in Three States." November 2, 1964.

Cleveland Herald. "Arresting a Monkey." August 15, 1893.

———. "A Snake in a Synagogue." April 30, 1884.

Colimore, Edward. "Searching for a Devil in the Deep Dark Woods: A Two-Centuries Old Legend Haunts the Pine Barrens." *Philadelphia Inquirer*, November 3, 2009.

Daily Inter-Ocean. "Children Stampede at a 'Witch.'" February 7, 1896.

Daily Ohio Statesman. "Frightful Scene at a Balloon Ascension in Philadelphia." October 1, 1851.

Evening Independent. "Phantom Radio Voice Gives Cops Case of Jitters." September 5, 1945.

Floyd, E. Randall. "Theories Abound Regarding the Mysterious 'Star Jelly.'" *San Antonio Express-News*, July 6, 1993.

"Furnace, Mill and Factory." *Engineering and Mining Journal* (April 4, 1885): 232.

Indiana Evening Gazette. "Another Pennsylvania 'Hex Murder' Seen with Finding Weird Symbol of Voodooism." January 21, 1932.

Jackson, Joseph. "The First Balloon Hoax." *Pennsylvania Magazine of History and Biography* 35 (1911): 51–58.

Meridian Journal. "Man Jailed Three Days in Hoax Not Bitter Against Girls." November 6, 1969.

Milwaukee Daily Journal. "Wild Steers Cause a Panic." January 7, 1890.

Milwaukee Sentinel. "Weird Ghost Story." July 13, 1890.

Mucha, Peter. "Jersey Devil Seen by Many, Reportedly Caught 100 Years Ago." *Philadelphia Inquirer*, May 22, 2009.

New York Daily Times. "Fall of a Wharf in Philadelphia." July 3, 1856.

New York Times. "Acrobat Dies from Effect of Fall." June 3, 1922.

———. "Alligator Takes His Arm." September 1, 1930.

———. "At Home in a Boiler." March 21, 1885.

———. "Balloon Party Missed Comet." May 22, 1910.

———. "Children's Hymn Averts Panic in Philadelphia Church Fire." May 14, 1928.

———. "A Circus Man in Trouble." March 29, 1889.

———. "Circus Manager Arrested." June 1, 1913.

———. "Circus Men Causing Trouble." August 27, 1885.

———. "Circus Wire Slider Falls." May 29, 1932.

———. "Crime's Varying Phases." June 10, 1879.

———. "Dead Engineer on Flier." February 7, 1907.

———. "A Director's Train Wrecked." March 16, 1880.

———. "Dynamite Caused Arrests." November 13, 1903.

———. "Eight Girls Killed in a Factory Panic." May 1, 1902.

———. "81 Hurt in Philadelphia Subway Trying to Escape Blast on Train." August 3, 1957.

———. "Elephants Fight in Car." November 24, 1902.

———. "Exorcising a Ghost." February 2, 1885.

———. "Fall from Circus Wire Is Fatal." January 4, 1934.

———. "Five Dead in Fire Panic." January 20, 1910.

———. "Ghost Answers the Phone." July 14, 1908.

———. "The Ghost of Clifton Heights." December 21, 1885.

———. "Injured by an Angry Lioness." January 24, 1883.

————. "Kills Mayor on Paper." December 4, 1910.

————. "Lifts Curse after 32 Years." March 1, 1908.

————. "Mourning Over the Wrong Man." February 25, 1878.

————. "Murderous Policemen." December 26, 1876.

————. "Philadelphia Sees Eclipse." May 24, 1910.

————. "Priest Averts Panic in Crowded Church." September 5, 1921.

————. "Saved Children and Died." May 9, 1910.

————. "Saw His Wife Married." November 17, 1901.

————. "Says Priest Restored Voice." December 31, 1904.

————. "Sentenced as Nazi Spy." December 6, 1945.

————. "She Says She Can Raise Dead." August 14, 1908.

————. "Struck Down with a Pitch-Fork." January 5, 1884.

————. "Ten-Minute Girl Strike." January 8, 1905.

————. "Tent Falls on 1,000 at Philadelphia Show." May 27, 1927.

————. "Think Dead Man in Trance." August 13, 1908.

————. "Told of Premonition and Died the Next Day." March 29, 1925.

————. "Treasure Trove." January 27, 1872.

————. "Twelve Foot Shark Is Killed in Delaware River at Tacony." May 1, 1922.

————. "Two Spaniards Held in Nazi Spy Plot; Secret Radio Traps Seamen at Philadelphia." June 24, 1945.

————. "A Victim of Witchcraft." December 21, 1885.

————. "Will View Comet from Balloon." May 20, 1910.

————. "Wounds 15 in Crowd Aiming at Bull." August 11, 1921.

North American. "Mad Dog at Large." October 31, 1888.

Observer-Reporter. "Scores View UFO in Skies over Philly." October 10, 1975.

————. "Zany Phantom Buried Alive." October 29, 1975.

Park City Daily News. "Blast Causes Panic in Philly Subway Tube." August 4, 1957.

Philadelphia Daily News. "Moon Tree." May 7, 1975.

Philadelphia Inquirer. "Electric Cloud Enveloped Ship." August 1, 1904.

————. "Hurricane Kills 15 in Philadelphia Area, Leaves Path of Ruin in 8 States." October 16, 1954.

————. "Saved Two Lives, but Lost His Own." February 13, 1902.

————. "Thought the Shadows Ghosts." May 24, 1896.

Philadelphia Press. "Explosion at a Meat Packing Establishment." November 11, 1861.

Philadelphia Telegraph. "A Girl Falls from a Trapeze." April 15, 1880.

Philadelphia Times. "Living with Part of His Skull Gone." March 27, 1880.

Pittsburgh Press. "Scores Injured in Subway Blast." August 2, 1957.

Republican Compiler. "Melancholy Occurrence." May 5, 1828.

Rocky Mountain News. "A Ghost in Philadelphia." February 12, 1883.

Spokesman-Review. "Little Early for Spooks." October 9, 1948.

St. Louis Globe Democrat. "Rattlesnake Joe." May 30, 1882.

———. "Shooting a Sewer." April 29, 1885.

Time. "Enemy Aliens: Asps on the Hearth." February 9, 1942.

Tyrone Daily Herald. "Negro Confesses to Part in 1932 'Hex Murder.'" April 15, 1937.

Williamson Daily News. "Halloween Story Is a Hoax." November 5, 1969.

Windsor-Star. "Pills for Candies, Halloween Treat." November 1, 1966.

BOOKS

Breuer, William B. *The Air Raid Warden Was a Spy and Other Tales from Home-Front America in World War II*. Edison, NJ: Castle Books, 2005.

McCloy, James F., and Ray Miller Jr. *The Jersey Devil*. Moorestown, NJ: Middle Atlantic Press, 1976.

Watson, John F., and Willis Hazard. *Annals of Philadelphia and Pennsylvania in the Olden Time*. Vols. I–III. Philadelphia: Edwin S. Stuart, 1884.

Weigley, Russell Frank, and Edwin Wolf. *Philadelphia: A 300 Year History*. New York: W.W. Norton and Company, 1982.

WEBSITES

"Historical Markers: Ricketts' Circus." Explore PA History. explorepahistory.com/hmarker.php?markerId=815.

Masks of Mesingw. masksofmesingw.blogspot.com.

"The Moon Trees." NASA. nssdc.gsfc.nasa.gov/planetary/lunar/moon_tree.html.

Project Blue Book Archive. www.bluebookarchive.org/default.aspx.

"Ricketts' Circus, 1793–1800." The Circus in America. www.circusinamerica.org/public/corporate_bodies/public_show/92.

Wall, Tim. "Moon Trees Being Lost? Time to Turn Over a New Leaf." MSNBC. www.msnbc.msn.com/id/41533855/ns/technology_and_science-discoverycom.

Weise, Elizabeth. "NASA Launches Search for Moon Trees." *USA Today*. www.usatoday.com.

About the Authors

Edward White is an associate at the law firm of Morgan, Lewis & Bockius LLP in Philadelphia. Edward received his juris doctorate from Villanova University School of Law and a BA in history from Saint Vincent College. He has resided in Philadelphia and its suburbs since 1999.

Thomas White is the university archivist and curator of special collections in the Gumberg Library at Duquesne University. He is also an adjunct lecturer in Duquesne's History Department and an adjunct professor of history at La Roche College. White received a master's degree in public history from Duquesne University. Besides the folklore and history of Pennsylvania, his areas of interest include public history and American cultural history. He is the author of *Legends and Lore of Western Pennsylvania*, *Forgotten Tales of Pennsylvania*, *Ghosts of Southwestern Pennsylvania* and *Forgotten Tales of Pittsburgh*, all published by The History Press.

Visit us at

www.historypress.net